Bogle L'Ouve

GW01418862

Socialist History Society

Socialist History
Occasional Publications Series No. 30

Caribbean
Workers'
Struggles

Richard Hart

2012

Published by Socialist History Society with
Bogle L'Ouverture Press, 2012

ISBN 978-0-9555138-6-2

Text typeset by SHS, 2012

www.socialisthistorysociety.co.uk

Contents

Preface

The Socialist History Society is extremely pleased to be able to publish this latest work from the pen of the distinguished lawyer, activist and academic Richard Hart. The author is a very familiar and much respected figure on the left in Britain and in the Caribbean for his consistent stand against imperialism and his advocacy of liberation for the peoples of Africa and the Caribbean, staunch opinions which shine through in all his writings. Richard Hart is a long-standing member of the SHS and he has spoken at public meetings organised by the society in London. He is the author of two earlier SHS pamphlets: *Labour Rebellions of the 1930s in the British Caribbean Region Colonies* and *The Grenada Revolution: setting the record straight*, both of which were published jointly with Caribbean Labour Solidarity. We commend his latest publication which we are publishing in collaboration with Bogle L'Ouverture Press, with a special introduction by Kimani S. K. Nehusi. We hope that this volume receives the wide readership that it deserves. We trust that it will inspire future research into the history and ongoing struggles of the Caribbean working class and organised labour.

The editors, on behalf of the Socialist History Society

Introduction

It is perhaps not at all inaccurate to refer to the Caribbean people, as C. L. R. James does, as 'unique in the modern world'.[1] It was in this region that some Europeans first decimated the original Native American owners to the point of near extinction. It was here, too, that capital was first mobilised into such dominance over labour that it was only the determined dignity of the latter which prevented enslaved African workers, who were made to succeed the Native Americans as forced labourers, from becoming mere units of production, no more than the property of their owners, alongside which it was common practice for them to be listed in plantation records. Yet, this was exactly how the workers were categorised, perceived and treated by their enslavers. Mass terrorism and dehumanisation of forced labour marked the order of that era.

But it was ultimately not mere physical force that kept the enslaved African majority permanently subjugated and freely available for the productive process. The system of enslavement rested just as much, or even more so, upon a collection of related ideas, values, attitudes and behaviour that were forcibly and consistently articulated by the dominant institutions of society including the church, administration, judiciary, police, legislature, newspapers and plantation. The latter was so dominant that scholars almost unanimously described it as a total institution. These official institutions demeaned, defamed and outlawed African culture, ethnically cleansed history of African achievement, and so assassinated African identity and ultimately disabled Africans in ways that still retard development. On the other hand, Europe was incorrectly proffered as the source of everything good; in a word, inherently superior. The majority of oppressors and oppressed alike were inculcated with these lies, and so a society was created where race mattered more than anything else in the determination of most people's fortunes. For it was here, too, for the first time in human history, that race determined class and the possession and loss of freedom – though not necessarily dignity – and these two factors coincided so neatly and so decisively in the shaping of society. The major contours of Caribbean society were erected during the period of enslavement.

Eric Williams[2] has led the way in demonstrating how the profits amassed from this evil system were deployed to launch the Industrial Revolution and the sustained predominance and material riches of Europe and most Europeans, and the impoverishment of Africans, as well as East Indians, Chinese, Madeirans and others, the majority of whom were later exploited, first as bound workers, after the legal termination of physical enslavement of Africans. This latter, often called emancipation and even freedom, happened in 1838 in the British dominated Caribbean, in 1863 in the USA, in 1880 in Cuba, in 1888 in Brazil, 1874 in Ghana, 1916 in Nigeria and 1928 in Sierra Leone. But nowhere in the Western hemisphere or in Africa did the end of physical enslavement mean an end to mental enslavement: that pernicious system of values, attitudes and behaviour referred to above. Nor has 'freedom', and later independence, ever meant an end to the exploitation of the working people, the vast majority of Caribbean society, and their consequent struggle for bread, justice and dignity. Modernity has been constructed, and continues to exist, upon these vulgar contradictions. Fanon,[3] Beckford,[4] Rodney,[5] Leary,[6] and others have shown us that the psychological, economic, social, political and other consequences of this hideous past, as well as the system of world domination that was erected upon it during that era, are still vigorously alive in the lives of all its inheritors, for it has been instrumental in shaping the fortunes of all who came or were brought to this region: Native American and European, African and Asian; rich and poor alike as well as those in between – and countless others beyond these shores.

It is therefore scarcely surprising that the Caribbean produced more than its fair share of fighters against this pernicious system, from those who specialised in physical attacks upon the oppressors and their property, to those who excelled at pen, art, oratory and other aspects of the arts, to those whose genius it was to accomplish a happy marriage of both. A supporting, validating, and even, on occasion, a valorising system of values and ideas is inescapably an aspect of both organised oppression and the liberation it invariably calls forth. Hence a contest of vision, values, ideas, attitudes and behaviour must necessarily accompany a people's struggle for liberation. It is for this reason that resistance, revolt and revolution constitute more than a subtext in Caribbean social history. This is a dominant theme clearly inscribed upon the region's consciousness from the very beginning of the period of European predominance, a constant opponent of the comprehensive and deeply rooted system of subjugation, for wherever there is oppression people will resist, since that is a measure of our common humanity.

But accommodation and outright capitulation have also marked the social relations of this region, for it is the full spectrum of possibilities resident in the human spirit that have played themselves out in the complex history of this place. It has not been unusual, though it is also true that it has never been so frequent as to be commonplace, for men and women of the privileged classes to be as equal as anyone else in their dedication to the fight against injustice, or for some of the oppressed to be recruited by the prevailing system and corrupted into working against the interests of their fellows. Here, a fierce hatred of injustice has never been the exclusive birthright of the oppressed, nor greed and other manifestations of moral weakness the special preserve of oppressors alone. Morality and immorality have resided side by side in the social reality of this region, and often in a single individual too. If inhumanity triumphed for a season, it seems that a common humanity residing among oppressor and oppressed alike regularly threatened to undermine that evil system, for decent and courageous people of all classes, races, creeds and genders have often made common cause against dehumanisation and other manifestations of oppression. This is a region whose sons and daughters often value freedom above privilege and honesty above power or its trappings. C L R James's observation that 'Liberty means something to us [i.e. Caribbean people] that is very unusual' is neither adventurous nor misplaced in his essay, referred to above, on the making of the region's people.[7] The most eloquent and irrefutable testimony to this fact of Caribbean existence is provided by the sustained dedication and help given to the independence movement of Africa by James himself, by Marcus Garvey, George Padmore, Ras Makonnen, Frantz Fanon and other Africans from the Caribbean and also by the theoretical and practical help to the African liberation movements by a

5

succeeding generation of Caribbean radicals, of whom Walter Rodney is undoubtedly the foremost example, who followed in the footsteps of Garvey, James *et al.* More evidence of an outstanding Caribbean commitment to human liberty lies in the relatively new and glorious pages in internationalist solidarity written – and still being written – by Cuban volunteers in the fight for freedom and dignity in the Caribbean itself, as well as in Latin America, in Angola, Congo, Namibia, Azania (South Africa) and other parts of Africa, in Syria, in Pakistan and in other lands thousands of miles away from this region.[8] The history of the Caribbean teaches us that race, gender and class are not the only markers of humanity, and that each by itself is neither an unmitigated determinant of nor an infallible guide to human character.

The origins of Fedon, Cespedes, Marti, Bolivar, Fidel and Raul Castro, Che Guevara and many others among the well-to-do may not at first glance appear to equip them for the careers by which they have distinguished themselves and helped to distinguish this region. Yet, in the roll call of the Caribbean's great radicals and revolutionaries, they are forever linked with Hautey, Makandal, Kofi, Atta, Accrabe, Boukman, Cecile Fatima, Marie Claire Heureuse Félicité Bonheur, L'Ouverture, Dessalines, Carlota, Nanny, Padmore, Fanon, Juan Almedia, Maurice Bishop, Walter Rodney, *los mambises* and countless other unnamed heroes who arose from the most oppressed sections of this society. In the same way, in Europe, the name of Karl Marx is forever associated with that of his wealthy and equally committed collaborator, Friedrich Engels. Surely, it was not class alone that determined character or career in any of these extraordinary people; they were each driven by a love of humanity that dictated a striving for humanist principles which transcend those more mundane divisions of class, race, gender and creed, divisions that limit the horizons of most other people and so restrict the possibilities of their action. But they were indeed unusual, and that is an important consideration in our estimation of both these illustrious people and the more usual mortals who are bound by the common limitations imposed by a narrow defence of those categories of social existence that we have come to consider as normal, and so inevitable, in our calculation of the human condition and our estimation of both oppression and liberation.

It is not that these exceptional people may have loved any less their particular class, or race, or gender or whatsoever interest group from which they hailed. Rather, it is that they loved justice more, for it is our common humanity that was the foundation of their vision and the inspiration of their action. They fought injustice anywhere, so they belong to all human beings. They overcame that peculiar and often convenient or even opportunistic blindness and insensitivity to the experiences, perspectives and interests of others that has afflicted so many who would fight, but only for their race, or their class, or their occupation, or their gender. Too often has history witnessed progress only when the progressives represent a specific segment of society, but part company with the fight for justice as soon as they believe their sectarian interests to be fulfilled. Thus may other injustices be left unchecked, the highest ideals of humanity deserted, and society once more blemished or even imperilled. These illustrious people understood that an injustice anywhere is an injustice everywhere. Yet liberation, like charity, begins at home. Who can really blame anyone who fights injustice, even when their fight begins and ends only at their own doorstep? The highest ideals are the toughest ones to pursue and to fulfil.

Richard Hart could have chosen to keep himself well away from the trenches of this glorious and divided society and yet make an honest, good and quiet living, as well as a grand life, from an exclusive and lucrative practice of the law. He had trained as a solicitor at an early age after being sent off to an English public school. ('There is nothing public about them', he says, 'they are definitely privileged schools'.) He was born into a somewhat privileged upper middle class family and possessed the right colour and the right connections – very valuable assets then, as still so often now. His father was a senior solicitor who held progressive ideas that were mostly tolerated because of his ties to the Jamaican establishment. Hart senior had published and distributed *Monthly Comments* at his own expense. It was an early periodical that carried features on Jamaican history, economics and current affairs in every issue. He had also written a book on the life of George William Gordon, one of the leaders in the 1865 rebellion against British colonialism and, not coincidentally, one of Jamaica's national heroes.

It was in his father's library that Hart junior found most of the books that made a huge impact on the shaping of his consciousness. His father had become a member of the Left Book Club, undertaking to purchase one book per month out of London. He had a significant collection by the time Richard returned to Jamaica in 1936. (This library would later form part of the initial basis of the University of the West Indies Library at Mona, Jamaica). John Strachey's *Theory and Practice of Socialism* was by far the most influential text in moulding a mind that would in turn play such an influential part in the shaping of the modern Caribbean.

It was a changing Jamaica and Caribbean to which Hart had returned. *Public Opinion*, a new nationalistic newspaper, had been started by O. T. Fairclough, who had worked as an accountant in the National Bank of Haiti, then returned to Jamaica in 1934. He had therefore had the experience of working in an independent African country and was a witness to the capacity of Africans and the dignity of self-government, if not real outright independence. Fairclough presented his credentials to the Royal Bank of Canada and the Canadian Bank of Commerce, but was in both instances denied employment because of the racist policies which prevailed, openly, at that time. He persuaded Norman Manley, who initially held the opinion that the problems of Jamaica were not political, to get into politics, form a party and work for self government. Also prominent in the launch of *Public Opinion* were Frank Hill, who was also later influential in the politics of Jamaica, and the progressive Englishman, H. P. Jacobs, a teacher at a secondary school in Jamaica and editor and proof reader for the establishment newspaper, *The Gleaner*.

But if law is his profession it is political organisation that is Richard Hart's vocation. It is true that he did not completely abandon the law, but the story of his life so far is an eloquent comment upon his real calling. A love for humanity and a corresponding passion for justice have led him to an acute concern for the region, a resolute stance against colonialism and a forthright attachment to the fortunes of the working people, by far the majority of the region's population. In the backward colonial circumstances of the Caribbean in the 1930s such humanist persuasions defined his as radical. He became adept as a political organiser as well as a writer and emerged as perhaps one of the earliest organic intellectuals of the Caribbean. It is not surprising, therefore, that Hart's trade union, political and educational activities alarmed the colonial authorities. He was regularly followed around and reported upon by the colonial police and banned from entering several Caribbean territories. These repressive practices reached a low under Sir Arthur Richards, British governor of Jamaica. Using his wartime powers to imprison people without trial, this colonial dictator, on 3rd November 1942, imprisoned Hart as well as Ken Hill, Frank Hill and Arthur Henry, his fellow trade union officers, in the local prisoner of war camp. W. A. Domingo and Samuel Marquis, two other anti-colonial activists, had already been imprisoned there. Protests from Sir Walter Citrine, then Secretary of the British Trades Union Council, and Sir Stafford Cripps, secured their release after four and a half months. The radical fortitude of Hart, Henry and the two Hills also earned them expulsion from the Peoples National Party of Jamaica in 1952. Hart was subsequently readmitted with much ceremony. The two Hills had also been readmitted. Author Henry died before Hart's readmission.

Richard Hart's political activity must not be separated from his writing; they inform each other and are but differing aspects of his involvement in the Caribbean people's struggle for liberation. He has written seven major books and numerous booklets, pamphlets, articles and papers addressed to both academic and popular audiences. He has won many awards and received other forms of recognition for his work. It is not merely the fact of his writing which has served to distinguish him, but his concern with the majority and his insistence on including their stories as his major subject. Scholars, teachers, the working people of the Caribbean and others further afield, in fact everyone with an interest in understanding this region, must be fortunate that in his nineties Richard Hart has given us another book. It is informed by over seventy years of observation, activism, reflection, scholarship and insight.

The struggle of the region's people for freedom, from the time of enslavement to the attainment of independence, is the central focus of this text. By subject matter and treatment it belongs to a relatively new and growing corpus of works that makes a radical break with the system of mis-education and faulty socialisation which provided Caribbean people with the history, geography, literature, values and worldview of Europe, and nothing valuable about themselves and their region. In making the story of the Caribbean people its major subject, this text aims to empower and enable the people at the foundation of Caribbean society, for it implicitly acknowledges that self-knowledge is critical for development and social transformation. Self-knowledge leads to understanding of one's condition and provides the self-confidence and desire to transform both self and reality according to principles, insights and objectives derived from one's own experience and culture, without excluding the creative adaptation of influences from outside. That is without any doubt the most meaningful demonstration of freedom – and the truest meaning of independence.

Kimani S. K. Nehusi

Chapter 1

The First West Indians

Centuries before Europeans first entered the region, the Caribbean islands were occupied by migrants from the American mainland. The first to migrate up the chain of islands from the South American continent were members of a tribe who called themselves *lucono*, which in their language meant 'the people'. But the neighbouring tribe called them *Arawaks* (meaning 'meal eaters') because corn-meal was a principal item of their diet. They moved up the chain of islands and occupied Cuba, Jamaica and western Hispaniola (now Haiti), though there are still Arawaks living on the South American mainland.

The migrating Arawaks were followed up the chain of islands by members of another, allegedly more aggressive, tribe who were known as Caribs, a name meaning 'man eaters' which gave rise to the word 'cannibal'. The Caribs, who gave their name to the Caribbean Sea, displaced the Arawaks in the eastern islands, in Puerto Rico and in the eastern half of Hispaniola (now the Dominican Republic).

The original inhabitants of these islands have come to be described as 'American Indians', or 'Amerindians', due to a mistake by the explorer Christopher Columbus as to where he was, when he landed in the Bahama Islands in 1492. Unaware of the existence of the Americas, Columbus had sailed westwards from Spain in search of a sea route to India. He thought that these islands, on which he made his first land-fall, were islands off the coast of India. That was why he called them 'Indies', the origin of the term 'West Indies'.

Following Columbus's first voyage to the so-called 'New World', Pope Alexander IV, or the Borgia pope, anxious to avoid the possibility of a conflict between Spain and Portugal, the world's two great Christian powers, issued his famous 'papal bull'. In this he purported to divide all new lands discovered or to be discovered between these two powers by drawing a line down what he imagined to be the middle of the Atlantic Ocean. He decreed that all lands discovered to the west of this line should belong to the sovereigns of Spain and those new lands discovered to the east of it should belong to the sovereigns of Portugal.

By allocating the Americas to Spain and Africa to Portugal he hoped to ensure that there would be no conflict between the two Christian powers. In 1494 the sovereigns of Spain and Portugal embodied the Pope's decision in the Treaty of Tordesillas. All this took place without consultation with the resident Amerindians and with no consideration of the fact that they naturally regarded as theirs the lands that they and their ancestors had inhabited for hundreds of years.

At the time that the Treaty of Tordesillas was entered into, the Europeans were unaware that the continent of South America extended so far to the east that a large part of it lay to the east of the Pope's imaginary line. Nevertheless, having signed the treaty, the sovereigns of Spain and Portugal decided to adhere to it. That was how the vast area which came to be known as Brazil became a Portuguese colony.

The Spaniards established colonies in the main islands of Cuba, Hispaniola, Jamaica, Puerto Rico and Trinidad, but paid little or no attention to the smaller eastern Caribbean islands. That was why, in the early 17th century, English and Dutch merchants were able to establish colonies in Barbados and the Leeward Islands, the French were able to establish colonies in Guadeloupe and Martinique and the Dutch too were able to establish colonies. After two centuries of Spanish occupation few Amerindians remained in the islands. Having developed no natural resistance to unfamiliar illnesses, such as the common cold, introduced by the Europeans, many had died. Others, unable to adjust to the labour requirements imposed upon them, had left for the mainland in their canoes.

By 1655 the English had grown sufficiently confident to decide to challenge the Spanish monopoly in the larger islands. When in that year an English invasion force was repulsed by the inhabitants of Hispaniola, it sailed southward and successfully landed in the poorly defended island of Jamaica. By 1660 the Spaniards had withdrawn from Jamaica, leaving the island in English hands.

As originally envisaged by the merchants who financed the establishment of the eastern Caribbean colonies and Oliver Cromwell who authorised the state venture in Jamaica, the settlers would have received small grants of land which they would have been expected to farm themselves, with perhaps the aid of a few indentured (contract) labourers and possibly a small number of slaves brought from Africa. These small farmers had been expected to produce coffee, cocoa and other tropical products for export to Europe. But when sugar became by far the most profitable export, the small farm concept was soon abandoned.

The technique of making good marketable sugar from the juice of the sugar cane plant had been developed by the Portuguese, first on islands off the west coast of Africa and then introduced and developed further in Brazil. There had been Dutch settlers in Brazil who the Portuguese had expelled in and after 1640. Allowed to settle in Barbados and other English colonies these Dutchmen and their African slaves had brought with them the Portuguese method of making sugar. That was how the sugar industry became established in the English (later British), and subsequently the French, Caribbean colonies.

Chapter 2

The Slave Trade

Sugar was not a product which could be produced on small farms. There had to be factory buildings with expensive machinery. There also had to be a large adjacent area on which the canes were grown. The reason for this was that the juice has to be expressed from the canes soon after they are reaped, otherwise fermentation sets in and they lose their sugar content. As no railways or roads existed in those early days, over which the cut canes could be rapidly transported for long distances, the canes had to be grown on lands adjacent to the factory. The production unit required a considerable investment of capital. It had to be a plantation with a large labour force. But where was this large labour force to come from?

Initially the settlers in the English colonies had relied for their supply of the few additional workers they needed to supplement their own labour on persons recruited in the British Isles who contracted, voluntarily or otherwise, to work as 'indentured' (contract) servants.[1] Some indentured servants were persons convicted of a crime the penalty for which was death or imprisonment, who had been given the alternative option of a period of indentured service in the colonies. Others were persons who accepted indentured service as a means of discharging civil debts. Others sold themselves into indentured service to the master of a ship bound for the colonies in return for a passage to a new country and a new life. Such persons were, however, not numerous enough to satisfy the needs of the plantations for labour, were not accustomed to physical labour in a hot climate and could not be required to work after expiry of their terms of indenture which did not exceed seven years.

For more than two centuries after the first development of sugar plantations in the region, the overwhelming majority of labourers for the plantations were recruited in Africa. Africans were numerous, they were familiar with agriculture and also they were accustomed to working in an equally hot climate. As West Africa was nearer to the Caribbean colonies than Europe, the cost of transporting them was less. Africans, however, had no need of or desire for employment away from their homelands. Their recruitment and transportation to the Caribbean region could therefore only be effected involuntarily and by force. This was the context in which Europeans revived the system of slavery which, with the passage of time, had ceased to exist in all parts of Europe except the Iberian Peninsula, and began the infamous Atlantic slave trade.

Were the plantation labourers enslaved because they were black (Negro) and the plantation owners were white (Caucasian)? Such an explanation is unlikely. Factory owners in Britain, motivated by the same desire for maximum material gain, did not hesitate to have children of the same racial stock as themselves working long hours in their factories. If white labourers had been available in sufficient numbers and could have been transported as cheaply, European plantation owners, if they could have got away with it, would have been no less willing to enslave them.

But although Africans were not enslaved for plantation labour simply because they were black, but because they were available in greater numbers and were better able to do agricultural work in a hot climate and cheaper to transport than Europeans, this does not mean that racial factors were unimportant or irrelevant. It was undoubtedly easier for the slave trading and plantation interests to justify the extreme cruelties and loss of life which slavery involved when those enslaved differed in appearance and complexion from their exploiters and oppressors.

The initial traffic in African slaves transported to the Americas had been to the Spanish colonies. In 1538 the Spanish Government began to issue individual licenses to traders to supply slaves, most of the licensees being Portuguese. Subsequently, instead of individual licenses, the Spanish Government introduced a system of granting a contract to supply slaves, known as the Asiento, to a single contractor. English traders who supplied slaves to the Spanish colonies and Portuguese Brazil initially did so illegally. With the establishment of English and French colonies in the islands and their development of the sugar industry in the 17th Century, the demand for slaves greatly increased.

In 1631 a company was granted a charter by King Charles I of England to trade in slaves. This company's right to deal in slaves was renewed for 14 years by the Protectorate in 1651. But in 1661, following the restoration of the monarchy, King Charles II granted an exclusive charter to a company of noblemen, headed by his brother the Duke of York and including among its shareholders Queen Catherine and Mary the queen dowager, to supply 3,000 slaves per year to the English West Indian colonies and the right to sell slaves to the Spaniards. Two years later the company received a wider charter which purported to place them in possession of all of Africa between Salee in Morocco and the Cape of Good Hope for 1,000 years.

In 1672 the Royal African Company, whose shareholders included the King himself and the Duke of York, acquired all the assets of the earlier company. But although they were supposed to enjoy a monopoly of trade with Africa, they were having problems with English interlopers. In 1690 the Royal African Company's exclusive patent to deal in African slaves was revoked and by 1698 private traders were permitted to operate freely in and out of Africa on payment of a duty of 10 percent of the value of their cargoes as a contribution to the upkeep of the company's forts. But although they had lost their monopoly, the company's revenues received a considerable boost in 1713. In that year the British Government was able to exert sufficient pressure on the Spanish Government to obtain the transfer of the Asiento, held by French merchants since 1702, to the company.

It is impossible to determine with any degree of accuracy the total number of Africans imported into the so-called New World as slaves. Estimates ran as high as 15 million actually landed in the Caribbean islands and mainland America. The total number transported to the Spanish American colonies was estimated to be 1,552,000.[2] The total number entering Brazil was estimated to have been 5,750,000.[3] The total imported into North America during the period that the slave trade was lawful was estimated at 1,920,000.[4] The total number of slaves brought to Jamaica was said to have exceeded one million, of whom some 200,000 were believed to have been re-exported. Many slaves were also imported into the other English/British colonies and the French and Dutch Caribbean and South American colonies.

The slave trade and slavery took a heavy toll in human lives. Initially the European slave traders had obtained slaves by raids on West African coastal settlements. The exploits in this respect of the British naval hero John Hawkins, whose partner in his slave trading was no less a person than Queen Elizabeth I, a relationship which earned him a knighthood, have been recorded in Hakluyt's chronicles.[5] The slave traders, however, subsequently realised that an easier way to obtain slaves was to form alliances with African potentates whom they supplied with arms and encouraged to make war on their neighbours. They could then purchase their ally's prisoners of war, thus obtaining a supply of slaves without having to fire a shot themselves.

Although there were some exceptional African rulers, such as Nazinga Mvemba, King of Bakongo, who refused to participate in such arrangements and in 1526 declared: 'It is our will that in these kingdoms there should not be any trade in slaves nor market for slaves',[6] most local potentates succumbed to the temptation to acquire arms and European manufactures in this way. William Pitt blamed the slave trade for 'those dreadful enormities on that unhappy continent'. Referring to a tribal war on the Kameroun River in the House of Commons in 1792, he declared: 'I have no more doubt that they are British arms put into the hands of Africans, which promote universal war and desolation'.[7]

It is probable that in the wars and raids to obtain prisoners for sale as many or more were killed as were taken alive. In five expeditions by the soldiers of the rulers of Bornu, a state in what is now northern Nigeria, in which 15,000 prisoners were captured for sale, 20,000 others were killed. But deaths occurred not only in battle. Sometimes as many as five twelfths of those captured by the Bornu soldiers perished on the journey to the coast.[8] Of wars in the hinterland of the so-called Windward or Grain Coast (Sierra Leone), where operations were on a somewhat smaller scale, the slave trader John Newton wrote: 'Though they do not bring legions into the field, their wars are bloody. I believe the captives reserved for sale are fewer than the slain.'[9]

The numbers of Africans who died during the transatlantic crossings were horrendous. Such was the greed of the slave traders in their desire to carry as many Africans as possible on each voyage that they packed their prisoners into the holds of the slave ships like sardines in a tin, with often fatal consequences. The records of the High Court of Admiralty reveal some appalling losses. In 1652 the ship *Constant Ruth* lost 90 out of a cargo of 207 slaves. The *Fortune* lost 132 out of 320 in 1678.[10] The *Hannibal*, sailing from Whydah to Barbados in 1693 lost 320 out of 700.[11] The *Brownlow* in 1749 lost 62 out of 218.[12]

Between 1680 and 1688, 23 out of every 100 Africans taken aboard ships in the service of the Royal African Company died in transit. The high point was in 1682 when losses sustained reached 29 percent of the total number of Africans taken aboard.[13] P. D. Curtin, in his excellent study of the slave trade, accepts this percentage loss (23.4 percent) as valid for the period 1690 to 1700.[14] The percentage loss of slaves in transit by slavers shipping out of the French port of Nantes between 1715 and 1741 was 22.2 percent. During the 1770s and 1780s the losses suffered by the Nantes slave traders were at the rate of approximately 15 percent. Over a period of 46 years the statistics furnished by the French author Gaston Martin show that Nantes slave traders, who bought 243,000 on the coast of Africa, delivered only 203,800 for sale at the end of their journeys.[15]

Evidence taken before the Privy Council in Britain in 1789 disclosed that the average mortality of slaves on the Atlantic crossing was 12 1/2 percent, plus a further 4 1/2 percent as the average death rate between arrival at the port of destination and sale. Estimates of the number of slaves actually delivered alive by the slave traders to purchasers in the Americas vary widely and there is no means of establishing a total with any certainty. Estimates range from as low a nine or ten millions to as high as thirty million. Losses of life at sea were not however the end of this tragic story. The Privy Council also heard evidence that, during the 'seasoning' of newly purchased slaves on the plantations, a process lasting from one to three years during which slaves were familiarised with plantation routines and discipline and taught to use tools with which they might be unfamiliar, the average death rate was 33 percent.[16]

Chapter 3

The Exploitation of Slave Labour

The economics of managing the labour of slaves were clearly explained by Karl Marx:

> When his place can be supplied from foreign preserves, the duration of his life becomes a matter of less moment than its productiveness while it lasts. It is accordingly a maxim of slave management, in slave importing countries, that the most effective economy is that which takes out of the human chattel in the shortest space of time the utmost amount of exertion it is capable of putting forth. It is in tropical culture, where annual profits often equal the whole capital of plantations, that Negro life is most recklessly sacrificed. It is the agriculture of the West Indies ... that has engulfed millions of the African race.[1]

A Parliamentary committee, investigating the slave trade in 1791, heard the witness Henry Coor, who had worked as a millwright on plantations in four Jamaican parishes for 15 years and had his own gang of jobbing slaves, make the same point:

> It was more the object of the overseers to work the Slaves out, and trust for supplies from Africa ... I have heard many overseers say, 'I have made my employer 20, 30 or 40 more hogsheads per year than any of my predecessors ever did; and although I have killed 30 or 40 Negroes per year more, yet the produce had been more than adequate to the loss.'[2]

Field work on the sugar plantations was intense and exhausting, particularly the digging of holes for planting the canes and the cutting of the canes when it was time to reap them. The incentive used to encourage hard work was lashes of the cart whip, which were freely administered by the drivers who were privileged slaves under the overseer's supervision. During crop time work in the factories was equally intense and the hours were long. The cruel pace at which slaves were driven effectively shortened their lives and this continued to be the case after and despite of legislation enacted in some colonies which purported to place restrictions on the severity with which slaves could be treated.[3]

John Newton, the slave trader, wrote that he had been informed by a consignee to whom he delivered slaves in Antigua in 1751:

> That calculations had been made, with all possible exactness, to determine which was ... the more saving method of managing slaves: whether, to appoint them moderate work, plenty of provision, and such treatment as might enable them to protract their lives to old age? Or, by rigorously straining their strength to the utmost, with little relaxation, hard fare, and hard usage, to wear them out before they became useless and unable to do service, and then, to buy new ones, to fill up their places?
>
> He further said, that these skilful calculations had determined in favour of the latter mode, as much the cheaper, and that he could mention several estates in the island of Antigua, on which it was seldom known that a slave had lived above nine years.[4]

Over half a century later, a survey made on eleven plantations in the parish of St. Thomas in Jamaica over the period 1817 to 1829, showed that the average life span of those slaves born in Jamaica was 26⅛ years, while that of those who had been born in Africa was 53¹/₁₅ years.[5] The effects of slavery are dramatically illustrated by the population statistics. During the period of approximately 150 years from the English conquest of Jamaica to the prohibition of the slave trade in 1808 'upwards of a million slaves had been introduced into the colony'. Deducting the approximately 200,000 believed to have been re-exported would make the number absorbed approximately 800,000 to which must be added the children born to slave women during this period. Of this number, when the slave trade was abolished in 1808, the number of surviving slaves in Jamaica was stated to be 323,827.[6]

By the time slavery was abolished in 1834, the total number of surviving slaves had been reduced to 311,070,[7] but the number of free persons of African and partly African descent was estimated to have increased from 9,000 in 1805 to 42,000. Thus the decrease in the total number of surviving persons of African and partly African descent, even without taking into account the many children born to slave women, would appear to have been well over 400,000 or more than fifty percent.

However, no sooner had slavery been abolished than the population began to increase. The census taken in 1844 disclosed that there were 361,657 persons of African and partly African descent, an increase in the decade following abolition of about 8,500.

So severe was the toll of human life exacted by the slave trade and slavery that it is not surprising that there was an adverse humanitarian reaction, much of it inspired by religious sentiments. To justify such a cruel and inhuman system, the slave trading and plantation interests had to find a rationalisation for it which would still the consciences not only of those directly involved but also the British public. To achieve this, the spokesmen for the slave trading and plantation interests developed and carried out over a long period a well financed brainwashing public relations exercise.

Differences in appearance and complexion between the enslaved Africans and their European oppressors made it possible for these spokesmen to popularise the idea that Africans were a lower form of human life or not human at all, divinely ordained to be beasts of burden for the white man. It was suggested further that if these inferior beings were capable of redemption, this could only be achieved if they were subjected to the control and discipline which their enslavement by the white man alone made possible. This stereotype image of the African, to which was often added the allegation that he was a cannibal in need of Christian enlightenment, was fostered in a variety of ways, ranging from popular ditties and cartoons at one extreme to learned pseudo-scientific publications on the other.

A clear example of the latter means of indoctrination is this dissertation on the Negro by the widely read slave owning planter-historian Edward Long who wrote:

> In general, they are void of genius, and seem almost incapable of making any progress in civility or science. They have no plan or system of morality among them. Their barbarity to their children debases their nature even below that of brutes. They have no moral sensations, no taste but for women, gormondizing, and drinking to excess; no wish but to be idle ... They are represented by all authors as the vilest of the human kind, to which they have little more pretention of resemblance than what arises from their exterior form.

After two further paragraphs of such caricature this author continued:

> This brutality somewhat diminishes, when they are imported young, after they become habituated to clothing and a regular discipline of life; but many are never reclaimed, and continue savages, in every sense of the word, to their latest period. We find them marked with the same bestial manners, stupidity, and vices, which debase their brethren on the continent, who seem distinguished from the rest of mankind, not in person only, but in possessing, in abstract, every species of inherent turpitude that is to be found dispersed at large among the rest of the human creation.

Next, Long dealt with the question of the African's relationship to the rest of mankind and to the lower animals:

> When we reflect on the nature of these men, and their dissimilarity to the rest of mankind, must we not conclude that they are a different species of the same genus? ... That the oran-outang and some races of black men are very nearly allied, is, I think, more than probable ... nor, for what hitherto appears, do they seem at all inferior in the intellectual faculties to many of the Negro race; with some of whom, it is credible that they have the most intimate connexion and consanguinity. The amorous intercourse between them may be frequent; the Negroes themselves bear testimony that such intercourses actually happen; and it is certain, that both races agree perfectly well in lasciviousness of disposition ... an oran-outang ... has in form a much nearer resemblance to the Negro race, than the latter bear to white men...

Finally, Long came to the question of what God intended for the Negro:

> Let us not then doubt, but that every member of the creation is wisely fitted and adapted to certain uses, and confined within the certain bounds to which it was ordained by the Divine Fabricator. The measure of the several orders ... of these Blacks may be as complete as that of any other race of mortals, filling up that space, or degree, beyond which they are not destined to pass, and discriminating them from the rest of men, not in kind, but in species...[8]

Slaves were being imported every year. They came from many different African tribes and nations. At the same time children were being born to the slaves in the colonies who at birth took the enslaved status of their mothers. Slaves born in the colonies were known as 'Creoles'. A typical example of how the slave labour force was made up is illustrated by a list made in 1804 of the 494 slaves on a large plantation in western Jamaica known as 'Good Hope'.

This list, part of a sort of census of the plantation labour force made in 1804,[9] was made just four years before the importation of slaves became illegal after 31 March 1808. It showed that 205 (47.5 per cent of the total number of slaves on this plantation) had been born in Africa, of whom 110 were males and 95 were females.

> Eboes 88; Coromantu 26; Chamba 24; Moco 11; Banda 11; Canga 9; Congo 8; Mundingo 8; Papaw 6; Nago 3; Macoco 2; Portuguese Congo 2; Gaga

These descriptions, though not always accurate, give us some idea of the locations in West Africa from which these slaves had originated. The Ibo (listed as 'Eboe') came from Nigeria. The Mundingo were mainly from Sierra Leone. The term 'Coromantu' (more usually spelled Coromanti or Coromantee) was at first used to describe slaves shipped from Kormantine, a place in the Fanti area of the Gold Coast (now Ghana) where the English slave traders built their first slave trading fort in 1634. Later this term was used to describe all Africans shipped from the Gold Coast. These included persons of Ashanti, Fanti, Akim and Ga tribal origin.

Chapter 4

Slave Resistance and Rebellion

There were several instances of those who had been enslaved rebelling against their enslavement during the trans-Atlantic voyage and in some cases even before the ships on which they were to be conveyed even left the African coast. The slave trader William Snelgrave, whose book was published in 1734, wrote:

> I know several voyages had proved unsuccessful by Mutinies; as they had occasioned either the total loss of the ship and the White Mens lives; or at least rendering it absolutely necessary to kill or wound a great number of the slaves, in order to prevent a total destruction.[1]

To guard against the possibility of slave mutinies, not only were the crews of slave ships much larger than would normally be required to man ships of that size but in addition elaborate precautions were taken. As the slave trader Thomas Phillips explained:

> When our slaves are aboard, we shackle the men two and two, while we lie in port, and in sight of their own country, for 'tis then they attempt to make their escape, and mutiny; to prevent which we always keep centinels upon the hatchways, and have a chest of small arms, ready loaden and prim'd, constantly lying at hand upon the quarter-deck, together with some granada shells; and two of our quarterdeck guns, pointing on the deck thence, and two more out of steerage...[2]

Slaves on the plantations offered resistance to their enslavement in a variety of ways. The lower forms of resistance included deliberate damage to property including livestock, dirt eating to induce illness and induced abortions by females to prevent the birth of children into slavery. Sometimes slaves absconded from the plantation to which they were attached not with the intention of permanently making their escape but temporarily as a method of bargaining with the plantation owner or his attorney.

The objective of slaves who employed this tactic might be to obtain a reduction in the severity of the conditions under which they were required to work, or to obtain increased rations, or even to obtain the dismissal of a particularly cruel overseer. Such runaways would hope to make contact quickly with some sympathetic free person who would not betray their whereabouts and who would intercede with the owner or attorney on their behalf. They would authorise such a person to assure the owner or attorney that they would return to the plantation and resume work if their grievances were redressed. Sometimes this tactic worked. It was however a risky course to adopt, not only because of the difficulty of finding some means of survival in a safe hiding place but also because, should the owner or attorney reject their demands, the punishment for running away could be severe.

On Amity Hall plantation in Vere, Jamaica, which normally had a complement of about 300 slaves, there was just such a problem. In April 1802 Alex Moir, the manager of a neighbouring estate who had formerly been an overseer on Amity Hall and appears to have been hoping for reinstatement there, wrote a letter to the mother and guardian of the infant absentee heir. He reported that the overseer at Amity Hall was treating the slaves with great cruelty and that as a consequence 'the number of runaways increased to an unexampled degree - there being no fewer than from 25 to 30 continually absent'. Several of these runaways had, he said, 'come to me with whom they are acquainted ...' A month later Moir wrote to her again:

> I here inclose a list of all your Slaves now runaways - many of them I have very lately seen, & they are determined to suffer death rather than return to their duty ... They declare that the moment any other person is appointed to the management of it they will return ...and when they have such a person ... they will behave as well as any Slave in the Island.

A subsequent letter informed the absentee owner's guardian that three of these runaways, 'worth to you, Madam £600 currency [have] perished of hunger in woods'.[3]

A higher form of resistance was evident in the case of other slaves, who ran away from the plantations with the intention of permanently gaining their freedom. Such escapes were made either individually or in groups, sometimes clandestinely and sometimes in the course of a rebellion. Rebellions and conspiracies for rebellion occurred frequently, particularly in the colonies where the production of sugar was the principal form of economic activity.

The Maroons were escaped former slaves and their descendants who had established their own free settlements. The word 'Maroon' was derived from the Spanish word 'cimarrón' meaning wild or untamed. It was initially applied to Amerindians who the Spaniards had been unable to subdue but later acquired the meaning mentioned above. Settlements of escaped slaves were established in the British colonies in the islands of Jamaica and Dominica and in the then Dutch colonies of Suriname and Berbice in northern South America.

In the 17th century there were rebellions and frustrated conspiracies for rebellion in (Old) Providence Island (Bahamas) in1635; Barbados in 1649; Jamaica in 1656, the 1660s, 1670, 1673, 1675, 1678, 1683, 1685, 1686 and 1690; in Barbados in 1675, 1686 and 1692. In the 18th century such rebellions and conspiracies occurred in Jamaica in 1702, 1704, 1718, 1720, 1760, 1765, 1766, 1777, 1795, 1798 and 1799; in Barbados in 1708; in St. Vincent in 1719; in Berbice in 1733, 1749, 1752, 1762 and 1763; in St. John, British Virgin Islands, in 1733; in British Honduras in 1765; and, in Dominica in 1791. All these rebellions were suppressed, but the two rebellions in Jamaica in 1760 were sufficiently formidable to threaten the colonial establishment.

1728 saw the commencement in Jamaica the First Maroon War in which an attempt was made to disperse the Maroon settlements and re-enslave their occupants, which lasted for ten years. In 1739 peace treaties were signed with the leaders of the undefeated Maroons in the two major Maroon settlements, which conceded freedom to their inhabitants and allocated lands for their use. Under the terms of one of these treaties the inhabitants of Accompong still pay no taxes today.

The rebellion in Berbice in 1763 developed for a time into a war of liberation. The rebel slave forces drove the Dutch northwards down the Berbice River to the coast and established rebel headquarters at Fort Nassau. From there the rebel leader Cuffee wrote to the Dutch Governor claiming the whole colony and signing the letter as 'Governor of Berbice'. Subsequently he proposed a compromise - that the southern half should be free and ruled by the Blacks and the northern half should be ruled by the whites. Subsequently, when Dutch reinforcements arrived and dissensions arose within the rebel leadership, the Dutch regained control. Berbice, and the Dutch colonies of Essequibo and Demerara to the west of it, were occupied by British forces in 1804 and ceded to Britain in 1814, becoming in 1831 the colony of British Guiana.

In the Dutch colony of Suriname, lying to the east of Berbice, escaped slaves were even more successful. There, in the interior, they were able not only to form several stable self-sustaining Maroon settlements but to establish them as free self-governing African tribal communities which the Dutch were never able to suppress or conquer. These communities still exist today.

The island of Dominica which had been claimed by France had been ceded to Britain by the Treaty of Paris in 1763, reoccupied by the French in 1778 and recovered by the British in 1783. While this contest between the European powers had been in progress, the settlements established by escaped slaves had continued to grow. By 1785 several Maroon settlements had been established in the mountainous centre of the island. Military expeditions were sent against and by 1786 most of their settlements had been dispersed and their leaders captured.

The island of Grenada had also been fought over by the French and British. The island had been ceded to Britain by the 1763 Treaty of Paris. Reoccupied by the French in 1779, Grenada was finally conceded to Britain in 1783, but many French residents remained on the island. In 1795 the mulatto plantation owner Julien Fedon freed his slaves and formed them and slaves from other plantations, together with some of the French settlers, into an army which for a time controlled most of the island. The British however regained control when reinforcements arrived and re-enslaved the slaves who had been freed.[4]

The most decisive of all the slave rebellions in the region took place in the French colony of Saint Domingue. It had commenced in 1791 as an ordinary slave uprising but over the course of the next few years had became a struggle not only against the slave owners and slave owning interests, but a struggle for national liberation from the metropolitan power. Led by Toussaint L'Ouverture the slaves abolished slavery and expelled the French plantation owners, expropriating their property. In 1798 Toussaint forced a British force from Jamaica, which had invaded with the objective of capturing the island, to withdraw. By 1804 the army of former slaves, led by Toussaint's successor Dessaline, had defeated the force sent by Napoleon to recover the island and restore slavery and proclaimed the establishment of the independent Republic of Haiti.[5]

British abolitionists, confronted by the well financed campaign of the slave trading and plantation interests to dehumanise Africans and demonstrate the economic advantages to Britain of the slave trade and slavery, made very little headway prior to the Industrial Revolution. The industrialisation of the British economy brought into existence a new social class of wealthy and influential individuals, the so-called industrial bourgeoisie, many of whose members responded favourably to abolitionist appeals.

In the pre-capitalist era, when a land-owning aristocracy supplemented by merchant interests dominated society and controlled government and Parliament, social relations were strictly regulated. In Tudor times, for example, prices of goods had been regulated and the granting of monopolies had restricted competition. Everyone had been born into his or her prescribed place in society and social mobility had been non-existent. One of the tasks that the burgeoning capitalist class had had to accomplish had been to free society and the economy from its feudal shackles, ensure the pre-eminence of wealth over birth and establish social mobility, freedom of contract and other bourgeois freedoms including even freedom of speech.

Having themselves had to overcome pre-existing feudal hurdles in their own struggle to become the dominant social class, it was hardly surprising that among the rising industrial bourgeoisie there should have been individuals who supported the abolitionist cause. Slavery was the ultimate in the denial of freedom of movement, freedom of contract and social mobility. Slavery, by its denial of purchasing power to the enslaved, was also a system which restricted the growth of the market for manufactured goods. Members of this new class of factory owners and their financiers brought financial support to the abolitionists who enabled them to publicise their cause and compete successfully for the support of public opinion.

In 1787 Granville Sharp, Thomas Clarkson and others, nine of whom were Quakers, had formed the Abolition Society. Although most were opposed to slavery, it was agreed at an early meeting of their founding committee, Granville Sharp alone dissenting, that they should confine their objective to achieving the abolition of the slave trade and not to call for the abolition of slavery. This they regarded as realistic in view of the then composition of the British Parliament and the strength therein of the West Indian lobby. Abolition of the slave trade was achieved with the enactment in 1807 of legislation which provided that, after 1 March 1808, it would be illegal to import newly acquired slaves into any British colony.[6]

Thereafter there was some delay on the part of British Abolitionists in starting to campaign for the abolition of slavery. The justification offered for this delay was that to do so would impede the British Government's attempts to persuade other nations to agree to abolish the slave trade. Eventually, however, in 1823, the Society for the Gradual Abolition of Slavery, popularly known as the Anti-Slavery Society, was launched. Thomas Fowell Buxton, the Society's leader and its spokesman in Parliament, explained its proposals for abolition in a debate in Parliament in 1823.

Though Buxton did not suggest an actual date, he proposed that there should be agreement in the House on a date after which all children born in the British colonies should be born free. Slaves alive on that date should however remain slaves for their natural lives, with this modification that the Spanish system of allowing slaves to purchase their own freedom or have it purchased for them should be grafted on to British law. Gradual as this proposal was, Buxton however agreed to withdraw it when he was assured that the Government was prepared to agree to support the abolition of slavery.

The Government's resolution, moved by Minister George Canning, in favour of which Buxton withdrew the Society's proposal, was as follows:

> That it is expedient to adopt effectual and decisive measures for ameliorating the condition of the slave population of his Majesty's colonies. That through a determined and persever-

ing, but at the same time judicious and temporate inforce-
ment of such measures, this House looks forward to a
progressive improvement in the character of the slave population, such as may prepare them for a participation in those
civil rights and privileges which are enjoyed by other classes
of his Majesty's subjects.

That this House is anxious for the accomplishment
of this purpose at the earliest period that shall be compatible
with the well-being of the slaves themselves, with the safety
of the colonies, and with a fair and equitable consideration
of the interests of private property.[7]

Both the original proposal of the Society and the resolution put
forward by the Government, which was adopted by the House of
Commons, would obviously have required a considerable time
for their realisation. Buxton's proposal would have needed at
least 50 years to run its course. For the requirements of the
Government's more nebulous resolution to be fulfilled, assuming
that Parliament could at some indeterminate date in the future
be persuaded that the character of the slaves had been sufficiently improved for them to deserve freedom, might have required considerably longer. Why did both the abolitionist leaders
and the Government adopt such a gradual approach to abolition?

To understand this it is necessary to appreciate that the
leaders of these advocates of the abolition of slavery were, for the
most part men of property. Buxton, for example was the owner
of a brewery, William Wilberforce was a banker, responsible for
financing many businesses. These were men who wished to
ensure that, unlike what had occurred in Haiti, the abolition of
slavery in the British colonies would take place from above by
peaceful Parliamentary means without expropriation of the slave
owners' property, disruption of the existing social structure or
alteration in the colonial relationship between Britain and her
colonies. Had the slaves not themselves expedited the process by
a series of rebellions in the first three decades of the 19th
century, there is no knowing how long the process of abolishing
slavery in the British Empire would have taken.

Slave rebellions in the 17th and 18th centuries had been
straightforward liberation struggles by enslaved blacks against
their white oppressors. If there was a political objective, whether
or not clearly articulated, it was to end the rule of whites and

establish black self-government. In the slave rebellions in the British colonies in the 19th century, however, the objective of many of the leaders had become more sophisticated. The realisation that there were persons in Britain and missionaries from Britain in the colonies who were in favour of the abolition of slavery and could be their allies had opened up a new perspective for the enslaved leaders in these anti-slavery struggles.

At the time of the slave rebellions and conspiracies for rebellion that occurred in the 19th century, the slaves were aware of the abolitionist movement in Britain. Much of the information they received was the result of denunciations of the abolitionists at the dinner tables of the plantation owners and managers, reports of which were relayed to other plantation slaves by the house slaves. It is also interesting to note that rumours were in circulation among the slaves to the effect that the King or Parliament had decided that they should be free but that their freedom was being withheld from them by the local slave owners.

One of the consequences of the spread of such information and beliefs was that the organisers of 19th century slave rebellions and conspiracies began to concentrate on the more limited objective of abolishing slavery. Slave rebel leaders were no longer motivated, as in earlier centuries, by simple hatred of all whites and a desire to be free of white rule. National liberation from England and the establishment of black rule virtually ceased to be part of the rebel agendas. In the Emancipation Rebellion in Jamaica in 1831-1832 many rebels had initially believed that they would only have to contend with the local militia and that British troops would not be employed against them.

When the British Parliament in 1823 accepted in principle the desirability of abolishing slavery, they had hoped, as we have seen, that the transition from slave labour to wage labour could be effected very gradually. Both the abolitionist leaders and the Government had envisaged a process the completion of which would have taken at least 50 and possibly as long as 100 or more years. Seven years later the members of the Anti-Slavery Society at their meeting in London, despite the disapproval of their leaders, approved a resolution demanding 'That from and after the first of January 1830 every slave born within the King's dominions shall be free'.[8] A mere 10 years later the British Parliament, reformed no doubt by the Reform Act 1832 which widened the franchise, enacted the Abolition of Slavery Act 1833. How are these dramatic changes of attitude to be explained?

Without doubt the most important factor giving the issue of abolition an urgency which, in the minds of both British abolitionists and members of Parliament, it had not previously had, was the intervention of the slaves themselves. Close on the heels of the abolition of slavery in Haiti and the start of the rebel slaves' ultimately successful war against the French force sent to re-enslave them, had come a series of rebellions and conspiracies for rebellion in the British colonies.

In Dominica in 1802 slaves enlisted in the 8th West India regiment rebelled and took temporary control of Fort Shirley. When the mutiny was suppressed 34 rebels were sentenced to be hanged.[9] In Jamaica a conspiracy had been discovered in Kingston in 1803 and the two leading conspirators had been executed. In 1806 a conspiracy discovered in the then parish of St. George had led to the execution of one and the transportation of five. In 1808 some 50 slaves described as 'Coromantins' and 'Chambas', who had been pressed into service in the 2nd West India Regiment, rose in revolt and killed two of the officers. In 1809 another conspiracy was frustrated in Kingston as a result of which two were hanged and several transported.

In 1815 a formidable conspiracy occurred in the parish of St. Elizabeth in Jamaica involving 250 Ibo slaves. In a letter to the Secretary of State for the Colonies the Governor mentioned preparatory meetings for the uprising at which he said that the object was: 'to impress the slaves generally with a belief that Mr Wilberforce was to be their Deliverer, and that if the White Inhabitants did not make them free, they ought to make themselves free'. The principal leader was sentenced to be hanged.[10]

In Barbados in 1816 there was a formidable rebellion. The number of slaves involved is difficult to determine but one reliable Barbadian historian has estimated the number as 3,900 males. He does not give the number of female rebels. Other estimates are higher. After suppression of the rebellion the Governor gave the numbers of convicted rebels as 144 executed under Martial Law, 70 sentenced to death and 123 sentenced to transportation. An anonymous contemporary author stated that 'a little short of 1,000 slaves were killed in battle and executed at law'. Here again there was evidence of dissemination among the rebels of the belief that they had been freed. A local newspaper informed its readers that:

> ...the principal instigators of this insurrection, who are negroes of the worst disposition, but of superior understanding, and some of whom can read and write, availed themselves of ... parliamentary interference and the public anxiety it occasioned, to instill into the minds of the slaves generally a belief that they were already freed by the King and Parliament.[11]

In 1823 a major slave rebellion occurred in Demerara one of the colonies in northern South America ceded to Britain by the Dutch in 1814. Some 13,000 slaves were involved. The rebel leaders do not appear to have had any plans for offensive action, their idea being that the slaves should refuse to work as slaves. This rebellion however received considerable publicity in Britain because of the fact that a sympathetic abolitionist missionary, who had been arrested and sentenced by court martial to imprisonment on a false charge of inciting the slaves to rebel, had died in prison. His death aroused more anti-slavery sentiment in Britain than the deaths of the many slaves shot and killed by the troops and the militia.[12]

The most extensive and important of all the 19th century slave rebellions occurred in western Jamaica in 1831-1832, involving some 20,000 slaves. Its inspirer and principal organiser was the slave Sam Sharp, a Baptist lay preacher who also had contacts with the so-called Native Baptists. Sharpe had a coherent strategy which involved a general strike against further work by the slaves unless the plantation owners would agree to pay them wages. Only in the event of their refusal to do so would they fight for their freedom. This second phase of the planned rebellion was to commence on a signal to be given by the burning of the trash house at Kensington, a plantation on a high elevation located near the St. James Trelawny parish border.

Here again it was widely believed by the rebels that the King and Parliament had already decreed that they should be free and that it was the local slave owners who were denying them their right to freedom. Whether Sharp, who was literate and highly intelligent, believed this rumour is doubtful, but he had it widely disseminated by his agent, a free black man who was able to travel widely. It was also initially believed by many rebels, until events proved to the contrary, that the British troops stationed in the island would not act against them and that they would have only the militia to contend with. The signal was given on the night of 27 December, 1831 when the uprising proper commenced.

The rebellion was crushed by the overwhelming military forces employed by the establishment. By the middle of February 1832 only small parties of rebels were still active. Two months later, when all effective resistance had ceased, the atmosphere was still reported to be tense in western parts of the island. In a report to the Assembly the estimate given of the value of the property destroyed in the five western parishes affected by the rebellion and an adjoining central parish in which disaffected slaves appear to have taken the opportunity to do considerable damage, was:

St. James	£606,250-0-0
Hanover	£425,818-15-0
Westmoreland	£47,092-0-0
St. Elizabeth	£22,146-9-7
Trelawny	£4,960-12-1
Manchester	£46,270-0-0
Total	£1,152,537-16-8

Small amounts of damage occurring in the two eastern parishes, which for some reason were also attributed to the rebellion, brought the total loss suffered to approximately £1,154,590. The expense incurred in suppressing the rebellion was estimated, with fine precision, to have been £161,569-19-1.[13] Multiplication by a factor of 50 would approximately translate these figures into today's money value.

Sharp was captured and was executed on 23 May 1832. Some 750 slaves and 14 free persons were convicted, in both the military and slave courts, for participation in the rebellion. By far the greater number of those placed on trial were sentenced to death. Other sentences were so severe that only the hardy could have survived. The Methodist missionary Henry Bleby, who interviewed Sam Sharp while he was in the gaol at Montego Bay awaiting execution, recorded his famous defiant statement that he 'would rather die upon yonder gallows that live in slavery'. Bleby also recorded the dignified way in which Sharp behaved when taken to the gallows and how many of the other rebels faced their execution:

> The undaunted bravery and fortitude with which many of the insurgents met their fate formed a very remarkable feature of the transactions of the period; and strikingly indicated the difficulty attendant upon the maintenance of slavery, now that the spirit of freedom had gone abroad, and many of the Negroes had learned to prefer death to bondage.[14]

Missionaries, particularly those of the Nonconformist churches, had a considerable influence on the slaves. The organisers and leaders of the major 19th century rebellions in Demerara and Jamaica were inspired by religious motivations. But despite the widely held belief of members of the colonial legislative assemblies that missionaries had instigated these rebellions, and the fact that in some cases their chapels were burned down or otherwise damaged or destroyed, the missionaries had advised their slave converts that they should not rebel or, by any means other than good behaviour, take any action designed to bring about their own emancipation.

The Methodist Henry Bleby, who had been physically targeted by members of the pro-slavery Colonial Church Union, cautioned his slave converts 'that even slaves were required patiently to submit to their lot, until the Lord in His providence is pleased to change it'.[15] The Baptist missionary William Knibb, who was opening a new chapel at Salters Hill in St. James on 27 December, the day preceding the night on which the signal for the uprising to start would be given, issued this stern warning to the assembled converts:

> I learn that some wicked people have persuaded you that the King has made you free... What you have been told is false - false as Hell can make it. I entreat you not to believe it, but to go to your work as usual. If you have any love to Jesus Christ, to religion, to your ministers, to those kind friends in England who have given their money to help you build this chapel, be not led away by wicked men.[16]

The Presbyterian missionary H. M. Waddell records that Knibbs's remonstration was not well received by his congregation:

> His assurances that no 'free law' had come for them, were discredited by the assembled thousands - his exhortations to be quiet and return to their estate duties enraged them ... They accused their ministers of deserting them; and the immediate destruction of all the properties in the surrounding districts was their fierce reply to his admonitions.[17]

Waddell's experience with his own congregation was similar. He recorded that:

> Before any blow was struck, I admonished my congregation on the subject. One with them, I said, in desiring their freedom, and not doubting they would yet receive it, I assured them it would come to them only in a peaceable and lawful way, - by the efforts of their friends in Britain, - while violence on their part would surely retard its progress, and perhaps insure their own destruction.[18]

It would appear, however, that the devoutly Christian leaders of the rebellion interpreted the scriptures rather differently to these their spiritual advisers, taking the view that God was more likely to help those who helped themselves.

The process of abolishing slavery in the British Empire was effected by legislation enacted by the British Parliament and the colonial legislatures. The Abolition of Slavery Act, enacted by Parliament in August 1833, provided that on 1 August 1834 slaves in the colonies should cease to be slaves and become 'Apprentices'. This meant that so-called 'praedial' slaves should continue to work for their owners at their existing work-places without remuneration for three-quarters of a working week or 40½ hours per week for six years. Any work in excess of the prescribed time was to be paid for at rates to be negotiated. All other (non-praedial) slaves were to be similarly bound for four years. Owners of slaves were to be financially compensated for their loss of human property at differing prices per slave fixed for each colony, but no compensation was provided for the former slaves.

It was within the competence of the colonial legislatures to shorten the period of apprenticeship if they wished to do so. The Antigua Assembly thereupon decided to dispense with apprenticeship entirely, all Antiguan slaves becoming entirely free on 1 August 1834. The Assembly in Montserrat decided not to follow the Antiguan example on the casting vote of the Speaker. All the other colonies accepted and tried to operate the apprenticeship scheme, but the apprentices offered so much resistance to what was essentially a continuation of slavery that they made it unworkable. Without exception, the remaining colonial Assemblies enacted legislation shortening the apprenticeship period for 'praedials' to four years. Slavery was thus completely terminated on 1 August 1838.

Was the abolition of slavery in the British Empire an entirely benevolent act on the part of the British Government and Parliament, as so many British historians have claimed? The rebellions and conspiracies for rebellion that occurred so frequently in almost all of the colonies during the 17th and 18th centuries and the Maroon wars in which escaped slaves in some colonies had defended the freedom they had won were a magnificent assertion of man's will to be free. They also provided a continuous condemnation of the system of slavery and a reminder of its injustices. But these rebellions had all been suppressed and the Maroon wars had preserved freedom for only limited numbers. Does this mean that the slaves made no contribution to their own liberation?

In view of the facts that the British abolitionist movement had proposed a scheme for abolition which would have taken at least half a century for its realisation and that the British Government, when it eventually concluded that slavery had to be abolished, had in 1823 devised a formula which might have required a century or more for its fulfilment, the fact that legislation abolishing slavery was enacted by Parliament a mere ten years later, does require an explanation. The conclusion is irresistible that it was the formidable slave rebellions and conspiracies that took place in the 19th century that made the British Government and Parliament realise that the abolition of slavery could not be delayed.

Referring to Sam Sharpe and the great rebellion that he led in Jamaica in 1831-32, Henry Bleby made this perceptive assessment:

> The revolt failed of accomplishing the immediate purpose of its author, yet by it a further wound was dealt to slavery,

which accelerated its destruction; for it demonstrated to the imperial legislature that among the Negroes themselves the spirit of freedom had been so widely diffused, as to render it most perilous to postpone the settlement of the most important question of emancipation to a later period.

The evidence taken before the committee of the two Houses of Parliament made it manifest, that if the abolition of slavery were not speedily effected by the peaceable method of legislative enactment, the slaves would assuredly take the matter into their own hands, and bring their bondage to a violent and bloody termination.[19]

Bleby's experience was limited to Jamaica and undoubtedly the rebellion there was the largest and most important of all the slave rebellions that took place in the British colonies in the 19th century. But the rebellions and conspiracies that had recently occurred in the other colonies should also be taken into account when considering what it was that turned opinion so decisively around in Britain. These rebellions were all suppressed but they nevertheless had a cumulative effect. By their rebellious activity the slaves had forced the British Government and Parliament and the colonial assemblies to set a firm timetable for the abolition of slavery.

Chapter 5

The Morant Bay Rebellion:
Paul Bogle and George William Gordon

Paul Bogle was a small farmer who lived in the village of Stoney Gut, about four miles from the town of Morant Bay in the Parish of St. Thomas in south-eastern Jamaica. He was the leader of a local native Baptist Church, which he and his followers had built. He had been 'ordained' by George William Gordon at the latter's native Baptist Church in Kingston. Gordon had been elected to the Legislative Council in 1844, but was not re-elected in 1849. He returned to the Legislative Council in 1863 as one of the representatives of the Parish of St. Thomas. Paul Bogle was his local election agent.[1] Paul Bogle was the leader of the popular uprising known as the 'Morant Bay Rebellion', which became a turning point in Jamaican and Caribbean history.

During the 1860s Jamaica, along with other sugar producing British colonies, was suffering the consequences of a decrease in the price of sugar exports. This was the result of the equalisation of customs duties on all sugars entering Britain. The cultivation of sugar canes had, as a consequence, been abandoned on several Jamaican plantations and this had converted the post-emancipation shortage of labour into a surplus. In January 1865 Dr. E. B. Underhill, the Secretary of the Baptist Missionary Society, had written to the British Secretary of State reporting the distressing economic conditions and the latter had sent a copy of his letter to Governor Eyre in Jamaica. To discredit the Minister's allegations the Governor sent copies of the letter to all the custodes, expecting them to denounce the allegations as exaggerated.

When the letter was published in a newspaper, there was an unexpected reaction. Public meetings were held in several parts of the island, at some of which resolutions supporting the allegations of economic distress were approved. George William Gordon, the elected member for the Parish of St. Thomas, chaired several of these meetings, at which he severely criticised

Governor Eyre as 'a bad man' who 'sanctions everything done by the higher class to the oppression of the poor negroes'.[2]

The Resident Magistrate for the Parish of St. Catherine stated that there had been a 50 per-cent decrease in the number of plantations in Jamaica since the abolition of slavery, which had created serious unemployment. This had been made worse by the importation of so-called 'indentured' labourers from India, to whom lower wages were paid than the hitherto prevailing rates. When a number of poor people in the Parish of St. Ann petitioned the Queen complaining of their poverty and asking that unused land owned by the Crown be leased to them on favourable terms, Governor Eyre forwarded the petition with a covering letter in which he commented:

> This is the first fruit of Dr. Underhill's letter, which represented the peasantry of Jamaica as being generally in a destitute, starving and naked condition ... and I fear the result of Dr. Underhill's communication and the circulars of the Baptist Missionary Society will have a very prejudicial influence in unsettling the minds of the peasantry.

No doubt influenced by the Governor's scepticism, the response of the British Government was unsympathetic. Eyre had the Secretary of State's reply to the petition printed on 50,000 placards, headed 'The Queen's Advice', and displayed all over the island. It read:

> I request that you will inform the petitioners that their petition has been laid before the Queen, and I have received her Majesty's command to inform them that the prosperity of the labouring classes, as well as all other classes, depends in Jamaica and other countries on their working for wages, not uncertainly or capriciously, but steadily and continuously, at the times when their labour is wanted, and for so long as it is wanted; that if they would use this industry, and thereby render the plantations productive, they would enable the planters to pay them higher wages for the same hours of work than are received by the best field labourers in this country; and as the cost of the necessities of life is much less in Jamaica than it is here, they would be enabled by adding prudence to industry to lay by an ample provision for seasons of drought and dearth; and they may be assured that it is from their own industry and prudence ... and not from any

such schemes as have been suggested to them, that they must look for improvement.[3]

The insensitivity of this published reply to the St. Ann petitioners and similar insensitivity shown to petitions from other parishes added to widespread feelings of frustration. At this time of widespread unrest and dissatisfaction, the uprising that occurred in the Parish of St. Thomas in 1865, although centred on local issues, could have occurred in many other parishes. Although this uprising has come to be known as the Morant Bay Rebellion, it affected a much larger area in the Parish of St. Thomas than the parish capital.

On 7 October a crowd of some 150 persons attended a session of the Magistrate's Court at Morant Bay in support of a man who had been charged with having allowed his horse to trespass on Middleton Plantation. The plantation was owned by a white man, who also held the office of Inspector General of Immigrants. He had leased the plantation to a farmer who had sub-let parts of it to small farmers. These sub-tenants were currently in dispute with him over the amounts charged for rent. The man charged, who was Paul Bogle's cousin, was found guilty and fined 20 shillings and had appealed with Bogle as his surety.

There had also been some disorder at the Court in connection with another case in which the Magistrate had ordered the arrest of a man for Contempt of Court, but the attempted arrest had been frustrated by the popular reaction. The Magistrate thought it imprudent to order further arrests on that day, but had subsequently issued warrants for the arrest of 28 persons, including Paul Bogle, in connection with the incident.

On Tuesday 10 October a police party attempted to arrest Bogle at his home at Stoney Gut. They were immediately surrounded by a crowd of some 300 men, armed with cutlasses and sticks. Some of the policemen had their own handcuffs placed upon them. One of the policemen subsequently stated that he had been forced to swear on oath: 'so help me God after this day I must cleave from the whites and cleave to the blacks'. He also stated:

> Paul Bogle spoke to the men in a language I did not understand. The men then took an oath, they kissed ... the Bible.

Paul Bogle gave each of them a dram of rum and gunpowder which they drank.

That day Bogle sent to the Governor a petition containing a warning:

> We, the petitioners of St. Thomas in the East send to inform your Excellency of the mean advantage that has been taken of us from time to time, and more especially the present time, when on Saturday, 7th of this month an outrageous assault was committed upon us by the policemen of this parish, by order of the Justices, which occasioned an out-breaking for which warrants have been issued...
>
> We therefore call upon your Excellency for protection, seeing we are Her Majesty's loyal subjects, which protection if refused to will be compelled to put our shoulders to the wheel, as we have been imposed upon for a period of 27 years with due obeisance to the laws of our Queen and country, and we can no longer endure the same.[4]

The policemen, who had been released and had returned to Morant Bay, also reported that they had seen three gangs of men, armed with sticks, cutlasses and lances, drilling near Bogle's house, and that Bogle and his men would be coming to Morant Bay on the following day. Alarmed by this news, the custodes called out the predominantly white militia volunteers to protect the meeting of the Vestry, which was scheduled to meet on 11 October. On that morning 22 armed militiamen from the company of the town of Bath and 8 from Morant Bay reported for duty.

That afternoon a crowd of several hundred, consisting of peasants, workers on local plantations and landless labourers, converged on the Parish capital. The largest contingent was from Stoney Gut. Led by Bogle and armed with cutlasses and sticks, they marched in a regular column headed by a drum and fife band. Similarly composed groups from other parts of the Parish also converged on the town. Bogle's contingent went first to the Police Station, overcoming the three policemen on duty. They freed the 51 prisoners and seized the station's stock of guns, but these turned out to be useless to them as they had no flints.

They then proceeded to the town square, marching to the beating of drums and the blowing of shells or horns, in three

'companies' of ten each and James Bowie, Craddock and Sim-
monds as Company Commanders. Paul Bogle had marched at
their head and they referred to him a 'General Bogle'. In the town
they were joined by people who had come from other areas,
swelling their numbers to about 400.

On being informed of the approach of the marchers, the
meeting of the Vestry, which was taking place at the Court House
under the chairmanship of the Chief Magistrate and Custos
Baron Von Ketelhodt, was adjourned and the members came out
onto the balcony. The Militiamen were drawn up in front of the
building. A large crowd of men, women and children had by that
time gathered in the square and Baron Ketelhodt commenced to
read the Riot Act to get them to disperse. He was interrupted by
a hail of bottles and stones thrown by women in the crowd. The
order was then given, either by the custos or by the militia
captain, to fire. The militia discharged their firearms directly into
the crowd. Before they could re-load they were charged by
members of the crowd and withdrew into the Court House.

The doors of the Court House were barricaded and the
shooting continued from inside the building. After this had been
going on for about two hours, a fire was started in the adjoining
school house and this quickly spread to the Court House. Some
of those inside jumped out of the back window while others ran
down the stairs in front of the building. When darkness fell, more
were able to escape, some taking refuge in a nearby house
belonging to a black builder named Charles Price. In all 18
officials and Militiamen were killed and 31 other injured. Seven
members of the crowd were killed and many were wounded.

The fact that Bogle's followers were under some degree of
discipline may explain why, apart from the burned out buildings
in the Square, there was little destruction of property and no
looting in Morant Bay. One of the militiamen, who had been
captured trying to escape and beaten, subsequently named
individual rebels who he said had been referred to as 'Captains'
and he said that he had seen them ordering men to march and
to stand guard at various locations in the town.[5]

The rebellion was basically a class conflict, though it
undoubtedly had racial overtones. This is illustrated by the
status of the prominent individuals attacked by the rebels.
Ketelhodt and Rev. Herschell, a member of the Vestry, were

plantation owners who had current disputes with their labourers over pay. Lieutenant Hall of the Militia was the Collector of Petty Debts at the town of Bath and was targeted by a man from whom he had sought to collect money. Vestryman W. P. Georges was a planter. Francis Bowen was a Magistrate and planter. Nevertheless, class divisions largely coincided with complexion differences and the rebels often articulated their protests in terms of colour.

William Blake, a black man who was associated with persons who the rebels regarded as their enemies, had a narrow escape. When a member of a crowd raised his cutlass to kill him, another man restrained him from carrying out this intention, saying: 'It is your colour; don't kill him. You are not to kill your own colour.'

The so-called 'Native Baptists' were closely associated with the rebellion. A white Methodist missionary reported, in a letter written to the Secretaries of his mission on 23 October 1865, that he had heard a Native Baptist say: 'You are black and I am black, and you ought to support your own colour. The blacks are seven to one of the others and they ought to have the island'.

Most of the white captives of the rebels in Morant Bay were killed, including Ketelhodt, Herschell, Walton, Captain Hitchins, Lieutenant Hall, Arthur and Alexander Cooke. But there were exceptions to the basic colour division. George William Gordon, who was not in Morant Bay when the Vestry met on that day, had a white father. Dr. Major, although white and a member of the Vestry, was spared to care for members of the crowd who had been wounded, but Charles Price, a black political supporter of Ketelhodt, was beaten to death.

On 12 October troops arrived and took control of Morant Bay, but by then the rebellion had spread to other parts of the Parish of St. Thomas. During the next few days it had spread as far as the border with the adjoining Parishes of St. Davids to the west and Portland to the north. William Kirkland, the Chief Magistrate at Bath and owner of a shop that was attacked, subsequently described the rebels who entered the town on the morning of 12 October as 'marching in ranks with flags flying, drum beating and a horn blowing'. A leader of the rebels converging on Bath was reported to have told the crowd: 'We don't want cloth, we want powder; we do not come here to thieve, we come to kill', but he was unable to persuade those who had taken goods from the shops to return them.

There was also widespread plundering by rebels who attacked various plantations. A white book-keeper on Blue Mountain Plantation was killed. William Miller, the manager of Serge Island estate, was concealed by a woman employee and was able to escape, but much of the plantation property was looted. Coley, the adjoining plantation, was plundered. Fifty armed rebels at Monklands were reported to have been looking for the owner, who had fled to Kingston. Others sought by the rebels were the Overseers at Golden Grove, and Amity Hall plantations and the Attorney at the former. A woman living on Rhine plantation stated that she had heard the rebels singing a song, the words of which were:

> Backras' blood we want, Backras' blood we'll have,
> Backras' blood we are going for, Till there's no more to have.[6]

Paul Bogle arrived at Monklands on Friday, 13 October, and appears to have been displeased that his strictures against looting had been ignored, but it is unlikely that he could have done anything to restrain the crowds of his impoverished supporters from looting. Plantations at Potosi, Holland, Amity Hall, Hordley, Duckenfield, Plaintain Garden River, Winchester, Wheelersfield and Mulatto River were all plundered and extensively damaged. The 'great-house' was however left intact and unlooted at Golden Grove, where people from Morant Bay had told the crowd that the house was wanted for General Bogle's use. They did however plunder the Overseer's house.

On the afternoon of 13 October some 50 rebels, led by John Pringle Afflick, marched into the small town of Manchioneal, then in the Parish of St. Thomas but subsequently transferred to the Parish of Portland. Armed with cutlasses and sticks, they were reported to have been shouting 'Colour, Colour' and blowing shells. They were soon joined by several hundred others. As the rebels approached, the white residents fled to Port Antonio. Among them was the Wesleyan missionary Rev. Foote, against whom settlers at Grange Hill had grievances as he had collected rents from them. Many houses were looted and the rebels took the guns they found in a local gunsmith's shop.

On Saturday 14 and Sunday 15 October a large number of rebels assembled in Manchioneal. According to the local gunsmith, their intention was to advance northwards into Portland on the following day. But this did not materialise. John Ashley Lord, a Police Inspector who was one of the refugees, believed that this was because they were engaged in pillaging and burning. Whether or not this was the cause, the arrival of troops on 16 October frustrated any possibility of a northward rebel advance.[7]

In view of the overwhelming forces employed in suppressing the rebellion, there was never any doubt that it would be crushed. On the morning of 12 October 100 black troops of the 1st West India Regiment, commanded by white officers, and 20 men of the Royal Artillery were landed at Morant Bay from HMS Wolverine, together with 74 seamen and 31 Marines. Governor Eyre asked General O'Connor, the officer commanding the British troops stationed in the island, for military reinforcements and 100 more troops were sent to Morant Bay aboard the gunboat Onyx. The Governor also requested that white troops from the military garrison at Newcastle be deployed and these marched eastwards over the mountains. On the morning of 13 October Martial Law was declared over the entire eastern county of Surrey (one of the three counties into which the island was divided). Later that day the Governor chartered a ship which took him to Morant Bay.

On 15 October Governor Eyre, accompanied by Colonel Alexander Fyffe, a former Superintendent of the Maroons in Portland and Custos of that Parish, met at Port Antonio with 200 Maroons, who had come to offer their services. These Maroons were poorly armed but, when HMS Wolverine arrived four days later, weapons and ammunition were issued to them.

It is interesting to note that Bogle had anticipated the possible danger of Maroons being employed to suppress the rebellion. About a month before the uprising Bogle and James Bowie had gone to Hayfield, a small Maroon community in the Blue Mountains above Bath. According to a Maroon Major, Bogle had discussed various problems with them, including the low rate of plantation wages and the high rate of taxes. A Maroon Captain said that Bogle had discussed the possibility of his going to the main Maroon settlement in eastern Jamaica at Moore

Town and had said that 'he was in fear of the Maroons because he was going to Court to have a battle and he ... wanted to go there and tell them not to interfere with what he wanted to do'.

The Maroons at Hayfield had offered Bogle no encouragement and it seems that he did not visit Moore Town. However, from the wording of the following proclamation issued by Bogle on 17 October, it would appear that he still entertained hopes that the Hayfield Maroons would support him:

> It is time now for us to help ourselves. Skin for skin, the iron bars is now broken ... the white people send a proclamation to the governor to make war against us ... we all must put our shoulder to the wheel, and pull together.
>
> The Maroons sent ... to us to meet them at Hayfield ... without delay, that they will put us in the way of how to act. Every one of you must leave your house, take your guns who don't have guns take your cutlasses ... Come over to Stoney Gut that we might march over to meet the Maroons ...
>
> Blow your shells, roal your drums. house to house, take out every man, march them down to Stoney Gut, any that you find in the way take them down with their arms; war is at us, my black skin, war is at hand ... Every black man must turn out at once, for the oppression is too great, the white people are now cleaning up they guns for us, which we must prepare to meet them too, Chear men, chear, in heast we looking for you a part of the night or before day break.

This was the last rallying cry of the rebellion. There was never a prospect of Maroon support. Indeed there was a skirmish with them at Torrington on 19 October. On 23 October Maroons captured Bogle and turned him over to the military forces.[8]

During the period following the suppression of the rebellion there was widespread indiscriminate retaliation against many members of the local population believed to have been sympathetic to the rebels. Hundreds were summarily convicted at Courts Martial at which no regard was paid to proper judicial procedures. Many arrests took place and Provost Martial Ramsay had many of those arrested and awaiting trial flogged. Many people were shot, hanged or flogged without trial at the whim of the military commanders, sometimes at the whim of ordinary soldiers or the Maroons. Over a thousand homes were burned down or demolished and there was looting of many peasants' homes by the military.

The case of a man named Fleming, one of the first of the prisoners to be disposed of, is revealing. He was tried by Court Martial at Port Morant on 14 October 1865, convicted and hanged. Referring to this case senior solicitor Ansell Hart wrote:

> Fleming at worst had been guilty of threatening, without injuring anyone. He had not been and was not accused of having been among the rioters in Morant Bay ... he was not taken in arms or in company of any others offering resistance to constituted authority. The offence of which he was charged had been committed, if at all, before the proclamation of martial law; so that his trial by court martial was quite improper.

Governor Eyre had personally set the example by ordering Fleming's arrest and trial by Court Martial. After his conviction the Governor sent a message to Lieutenant Brand to bring a rope for the hanging.[9]

Governor Eyre took advantage of the emergency created by the Morant Bay Rebellion to get rid of George William Gordon, his most persistent critic in the legislature. Although Gordon was in Kingston at the time, nowhere near the scene of the Rebellion, Governor Eyre had, on 17 October, personally secured a warrant for his arrest and had had him transported by ship into the martial law area. There he was tried by court martial. The charges against him were drawn up by General Nelson, pursuant to directions from Governor Eyre:

> For that, before the insurrection at Morant Bay, on the 11th day of October 1865, when the said George William Gordon did, in furtherance of the said massacre, at divers periods previously to the same, incite and advise with certain of the insurgents, thereby by his influence, tending to cause the riot whereby many of her Most Gracious Majesty's subjects lost their lives when assembled in lawful consideration of parochial and other matters – the said George William Gordon is arraigned: First on the charge of high treason against Her Majesty Queen Victoria; Second, with having complicity with certain parties who were engaged in the rebellion, riot

or insurrection at Morant Bay on the 11th day of October 1865.[10]

General Nelson appointed a Court Martial consisting of two lieutenants and a captain to try Gordon and they disposed of the case in less than half an hour, allowing the prisoner neither the opportunity to obtain legal advice nor to be represented by a lawyer. No credible evidence was given implicating Gordon in the rebellion. The sentence was:

> The Court ... adjudge the prisoner ... to be hanged by the neck until he be dead, at what time and place the Brigadier General may direct.

General Nelson readily confirmed the sentence and decided that Gordon should be hanged on 23 October. The sentence was accordingly carried out.

Paul Bogle was also summarily convicted by Court Martial and was hanged on 25 October 1865. Hanged at the same time were Bogle's brother, Moses Bogle and James Bowie and McLaren. According to a military eye-witness, Paul Bogle went calmly and bravely to his death.[11] In 1977, on the initiative of Jamaican Prime Minister Michael Manley, the Governor General awarded the title of National Hero to both George William Gordon and Paul Bogle. A monument to them was erected at Heroes Circle in Kingston. The building in which the Jamaican legislature now meets was named 'Gordon House' in his honour. A postage stamp was issued bearing the likeness of Paul Bogle.

There was an unfortunate negative consequence of the Morant Bay Rebellion, which was to have Caribbean-wide repercussions. The occurrence of that uprising made the British imperialists appreciate the rising influence and power of the popular masses in the colonies. They foresaw the possibility that the time would come when it would be impossible to resist demands for the extension of the franchise (then available to only a small minority of the adult population). The British Government therefore conceived the idea of persuading the upper social classes in the internally self-governing colonies to surrender their constitutions and accept instead the 'Crown Colony' system of government. This was a system which had already been introduced in the more recently acquired colonies of Trinidad and St. Lucia. Crown Colony Government required the vesting of ultimate control of both external and internal affairs in the British Government.

The persuasive argument was that the introduction of a crown colony constitution would not only facilitate imperialist interests but also enable the British Government to protect the resident upper social classes from the growing influence and power of their own workers and lower middle classes. When such a constitutional transition was proposed to the legislature in Jamaica, there was little disagreement and the surrender of internal self government took place with very little resistance. On 21 December 1865 the Assembly and the Council in Jamaica approved a Bill, the second clause of which read:

> In place of the Legislature abolished by the first section of the recited act, it shall be lawful for her majesty the Queen to create and constitute a government for this island in such form, and with such powers as to her Majesty may best seem fitting, and from time to time alter or amend such government.[12]

The Jamaican legislature having so readily agreed to the surrender of the long standing internally self-governing constitution, the other older colonies, except Barbados and the Bahamas, followed Jamaica's example. The Assembly of Dominica surrendered that island's constitution in the same year. In 1866 similar surrenders took place in Antigua, St. Kitts, Nevis, Montserrat and the British Virgin Islands. Similar surrenders took place in St. Vincent in 1867 and in Grenada and St. Vincent in 1876, but in the Leeward Islands the constitutions were amended rather than abolished. The St. Kitts and Nevis legislatures abolished elections entirely. Those in Antigua and Dominica initially retained elected minorities but in 1898, in return for financial assistance from Britain, elections were abolished.

Chapter 6

Labour: Unrest and Organisation

What could be described as three distinct waves of labour unrest and organisation swept across the English-speaking Caribbean. The first wave, which affected British Guiana, Jamaica and Trinidad, commenced in the late 1890s and had subsided by the beginning of the First World War in 1914. The second wave, which affected more territories, commenced towards the end of the First World War but had again subsided by the mid 1920s. There was also a discernible but short-lived after ripple in Jamaica from 1929 to 1931.

One of the factors fuelling the start of the second wave was increases in the prices of imported foods, which occurred as a consequence of the war. A secondary cause was the disillusionment which followed in the wake of reports of racial discrimination against black soldiers recruited for service in the war, the post-war repatriation of disillusioned soldiers and the disappointment experienced when insufficient assistance was given to help them to re-establish themselves on their return. The third wave, which started in 1934 and swept across almost the entire region, was fuelled by economic distress and a growing national awareness of events in the outside world. Unlike the two previous waves, this wave did not subside but gave rise to the modern trade union movements and the political organisations which pursued the quest of achieving political independence.

At the turn of the century, when the first labour organisations in the English-speaking Caribbean Area made their appearance, all these countries were British colonies. The English common law applied as did many British statutes. They all had their local legislatures which could, by statute, modify the common law. But prior to the Colonial Laws Validity Act of 1865 statutes enacted by the colonial legislatures were invalid if they were inconsistent with British legislation. This Act removed that disability. British statutes could however be specifically applied to the colonies if they contained a provision to that effect. Thus the legal position after 1865 was that the English common law applied unless and until modified by a local statute.

Under the common law organisations deemed to be in restraint of trade, including organisations formed for the purpose of regulating wages, had been illegal. This had been fortified by the Combination Acts, which made such an organisation a criminal conspiracy. The Combination Acts were, however, repealed by the British Parliament in 1824. Some trade unions were then formed although doubts persisted as to their legality. But in most West Indian colonies, following the abolition of slavery and apprenticeship in 1838, statutes were enacted reinforcing the common law. The preamble to Law 15 of 1839 in Jamaica, for example, read:

> ...all combinations for fixing the wages of labour and for regulating and controlling the mode of carrying on manufacture, trade or business, or the cultivation of any plantation ... are injurious to trade and commerce, dangerous to the tranquillity of the country and especially prejudicial to the interest of all concerned in them...[1]

In 1871 the British Parliament enacted the Trade Union Act which made trade unions legal in Britain but the Criminal Law Amendment Act of that same year imposed restraints on strikes and picketing. These restraints were, however, removed by the Trade Union Act 1875 which provided that:

> An agreement or combination by two or more persons to do or procure to be done any act in contemplation or furtherance of a trade dispute between employers and workmen shall not be indictable as a conspiracy if such act committed by one person would not be punishable as a crime. The Act specifically authorised peaceful picketing but certain acts of intimidation were forbidden with heavy penalties. It also protected the funds of trade unions from actions for breach of contract or tort.[2]

However, this British legislation was not made applicable to the colonies and, as a consequence, trade unions continued to be illegal in the English-speaking Caribbean Area. In 1909, following the emergence in Jamaica of some trade unions as affiliates of the American Federation of Labour, an attempt was made by S. A. G. Cox, a progressive member of the Legislative Council, to persuade the Fabian Socialist Governor Lord Olivier to introduce trade union enabling legislation. Olivier referred the matter to the Colonial Office where a senior civil servant endorsed the following memo on his despatch:

> This movement is apparently being engineered by the 'American Federation of Labour' and if it is successful, will mean that any unions formed in Jamaica will be controlled by the American organisation, thus leading to a further development of the Americanisation of Jamaica, which we are trying to hinder in other directions. Setting aside any question of its merits as a matter between employer and employed, I think it is on this ground a dangerous movement which we should not help forward if we can avoid it.

This cunning civil servant went on to point out that if Mr. Cox were to be reminded that he could raise the matter himself in the legislature, the proposal would be killed there if he did so. The author of this memo was relying on the reactionary composition of the Legislative Council, to most of whose members a proposal to legalise trade unions would 'probably be objectionable ... on other grounds'. The Secretary of State accepted his advice.[3]

The first organisation in the region, to be organised for the purpose of representing manual workers and others, was the Trinidad Workingmen's Association formed in 1897. It sought to represent both the skilled tradesmen and unskilled workers and, at the same time, put forward popular democratic and nationalistic political proposals. Its original leadership was petty bourgeois. The first President was Walter Mills, described as a druggist - that is, a chemist or pharmacist who owned a small drug store not a drug pusher or addict. He was succeeded by another druggist Alfred Richards.

In 1906 the TWA sought affiliation to the British Labour Party, but this was rejected by Ramsay Macdonald on the ground that its constitution did not provide for external affiliations. By 1914 internal dissensions had developed between Richards, whose orientation was mainly political, and other leading members, led by the stevedore James Braithwaite, who were more orientated towards issues of wages and working conditions. Another leader of this faction was Sidney De Bourg, a radical commission agent who had migrated from Grenada in the 1880s. But the atmosphere created by the outbreak of war was not conducive to radical activities and, though it was not formally dissolved, the TWA became inactive.

In Jamaica the first organisations representing manual workers were trade unions of skilled tradesmen. In 1898 the Carpenters, Bricklayers and Painters Union, popularly known as the Artisans Union, was formed. Its first officers were E. L. McKenzie, a carpenter, President, G. T. Atkinson, Treasurer and S. A. Phillips, Secretary. The latter was succeeded by W. E. Hinchcliffe, a carpenter. In 1901 McKenzie assisted in the formation of the Tailors and Shoemakers Union.[4] Although these unions were illegal there were no prosecutions, possibly because they were registered under the Friendly Societies Law or because there might have been protests as unions were recognised in Britain.

The first organisation of employees in Jamaica had been the Jamaica Union of Teachers, formed on 30 March 1894. Initially it was more of a professional association than a trade union, which it later became. At first it chose the European co-principal of the teachers training college as its President. Not until 1903 did its chief moving spirit, W. F. Bailey, a head teacher at a rural school, become President.[5]

In 1907 the printers organised a trade union, patterned on the American trade union affiliated to the American Federation of Labour of which it was a part. There were sections for compositors, pressmen and bookbinders with their own officers and an over-all organiser. Leading members included Nathan Campbell, Marcus Garvey and Edward Valentine (compositors), Tyson (pressman), E. N. Blair, McDonald and A. J. McGlashan (book binders). The organiser was Gregory. In 1908 this union called a strike which lasted for four weeks but was broken. Most of the leading members were victimised and the Union was destroyed.[6]

Also in 1907 cigar and cigarette makers formed a trade union affiliated to the American Federation of Labour. The leaders were Hunt, Mamby and E. A. Bain Alves, a cigar maker. This Union too ceased to function after an unsuccessful strike in 1908.[7] Hinchcliffe also was active in 1907 in a union called the Jamaica Trades and Labour Union, affiliated to the American Federation of Labour as Local 12575. In a speech reported in a local newspaper some years later Hinchcliffe said that this Union ceased to function in 1909. He said that because its most 'zealous' members, 'through circumstances had to migrate, some to Haiti, some to Colon [Panama], others to Port Limon [Costa Rica], the society consequently ceased operations'.[8]

In British Guiana (now Guyana) organisational initiatives were taken by artisans towards the end of the 19th century. In 1888 a Bakers Association was formed. In 1890 E. A. Trotz, a carpenter, is said to have assisted in the formation of a Guianese Patriotic Club and Mechanics Union, though no information as to the nature of this organisation has been found. In 1897 Trotz and others presented a Petition to the Royal Commission of that year, signed by 200 carpenters, masons, engineers, brick-layers, builders, porters and carters, complaining of lack of job opportunities and high taxation on essential food imports.

Unrest was also reported in 1890 among lightermen, stevedores, coopers and bakers and the press reported 'an epidemic of strikes'. The greatest and most militant unrest however occurred among the unskilled indentured and other workers in the sugar industry. There were strikes on sugar plantations in 1886, 1887, 1888, 1896, 1903, 1904 and 1905. Many Indian indentured labourers were shot dead, many were wounded and there were many arrests. In 1905, when field and factory workers of African descent were also involved in the strikes, they too were among the dead, wounded and arrested. Strike leaders included two women, Jungali of Plantation Non Pareil and Salamea of Plantation Friends. Robert Chapman, a factory worker strike leader on Plantation Ruimveldt, was shot dead in 1905 and George Henry, a field worker, was sentenced to six months imprisonment and a flogging.[9]

In 1906, the stevedores and longshoremen in Georgetown came out in a strike which had been secretly planned and well organised and took the shippers by surprise. Their leader was H. N. Critchlow, a stevedore. Though initially successful in halting all loading and unloading of ships, the strike was eventually broken. According to Chase, the effect of the failure of the waterfront workers strikes of 1905 and 1906 to win appreciable improvements and the ruthless suppression of the sugar workers strikes in 1905 reduced the workers to 'a state of passivity for about ten years' and no trade unions emerged. But lessons had been learned from the 1906 waterfront strike and Critchlow was later to emerge as the principal trade union leader.[10]

As the first wave of labour unrest and organisation subsided by the start of World War I, what had this trial run produced? In Trinidad the first organisation had endeavoured to enrol skilled and unskilled workers and to act both as an organisation representing the workers and as a vehicle for expression of political demands of a democratic and nationalistic nature. An attempt to affiliate to the British Labour Party had been rebuffed but an arrangement had been made with a Labour MP to raise issues in the British House of Commons. By 1914 the organisation, though not formally dissolved, had become inactive.

In Jamaica skilled tradesmen had organised trade unions affiliated to the American Federation of Labour. Unsuccessful strikes of printers and cigar makers had occurred, leading to victimisations and the destruction of their unions. Some of the leaders of the trade union movement had felt obliged to migrate to Latin American countries. All the organisations formed to represent employees during this period, except for the Jamaica Union of Teachers, were defunct by 1909. No attempt had been made to organise agricultural and other unskilled manual workers.

No labour organisations had as yet emerged in Barbados, the Leeward Islands, the Windward Islands or British Honduras (now Belize). There had also been labour, and in some cases peasant, unrest at the turn of the century in St. Vincent in 1891, Dominica in 1893 and 1898, British Honduras in 1894, St. Kitts in 1896 and Montserrat in 1898, but this had not resulted in the formation of labour organisations in these territories during this, the first wave of labour unrest.[11]

At the end of December 1916 a petition advocating wage increases and a reduction of working hours, signed by 585 petitioners, was presented to the legislature. The petition was the traditional Guianese way of organising support for popular demands. As the New Year advanced popular support for the petition's demands grew. In January 1917 Railway workers and waterfront workers in Georgetown came out on strike. Strikes also occurred in the country's second city New Amsterdam and strikes of sugar workers on plantations in Berbice followed.

Critchlow organised a new petition specifically directed to obtaining a general wage increase. Popular support for this was so tremendous that the Chamber of Commerce advised employers to concede a ten percent increase, which most of the big employers did. This greatly increased Critchlow's prestige. In 1918 he organised another popular petition, this time in support of an eight hour working day.

Faced with this demand the big employers decided that Critchlow must be stopped. He was accordingly dismissed and black-listed on the wharves. This led to a massive demonstration and march to Government House where the leaders were received by the Governor who advised the formation of a trade union. The British Guiana Labour Union was launched immediately, with Critchlow as its General Secretary.

The union was weakened by internal dissension in the early 1920s when a group of prominent middle class people with a reformist political orientation endeavoured to oust Critchlow. Financial support declined to the point that the union was unable to meet its mortgage payments and lost its headquarters. It recovered somewhat when this leadership challenge had been repulsed and a new mood of working class militancy developed in 1924 leading to widespread strikes in the capital. However, as the employers stood firm and no appreciable benefits accrued to the workers, the militancy receded and the recovery of the union slowed. Nevertheless, the BG Labour Union was the only trade union in the region, formed during the second wave of working class unrest, to survive into the 1930s.[12]

In Jamaica unrest commenced in 1917 which was much more widespread than that which had occurred during the first organisational period ending in 1909. The first strike in 1917, at the Kingston Ice Factory, led to arrests and imprisonments.[13] In that same year Bain Alves led another tobacco workers' strike which, this time, was successful.[14]

In 1918 a wave of spontaneous strikes occurred in Kingston involving many categories of workers and including employees of the Fire Brigade, longshoremen, coal heavers and sanitation workers. Even some policemen, teachers and civil servants came out on strike. The policemen's grievances were hurriedly attended to. Strikes of sugar workers also occurred in Vere, where three strikers were shot and killed, and in St. Thomas. These led to the appointment by the Government of a Conciliation Board.[15]

One of the most successful strikes in 1918 was at the Jamaica Government Railway, led by P. A. Aiken, Cyril Ivey, Edward Reid and other Railway workers. Out of this, early in 1919, the Workingmen's Cooperative Association was formed. Although open to other categories, its membership consisted mainly of Railway workers. It was registered under the Friendly Societies Law as they had been advised that a trade union would be illegal. As Aiken described it, it was 'a union under cover'.[16] Later that year the Government, responding to the tremendous labour upsurge that was still in progress, enacted the Trade Union Law which legalised trade unions. Following the enactment of this Law, Bain Alves assisted several other groups of workers to form trade unions, of each of which he became President These included, in addition to the Cigar Makers Union, unions of longshoremen, coal heavers and banana carriers, match factory workers, and hotel and bar employees.

These unions were grouped together in the Jamaica Federation of Labour under Bain Alves' presidency. A. J. McGlashan, veteran of the 1908 printers' strike, was the Vice President and effective leader of the Barmen, Barmaids and Hotel Employees Union.[17] Another veteran of the first wave of labour activity who surfaced again in the immediate aftermath of the First World War was W. E. Hinchcliffe. In 1918 he was reported by a local newspaper to be engaged in organising workers in the building trade in a union chartered by the American Federation of Labor as local No. 16203.[18]

By the late 1920s all these trade unions formed in Jamaica after the First World War had ceased to function. In or about the latter part of 1929 or early in 1930 S. M. DeLeon was engaged in organising a trade union called the Jamaica Workers and Labourers Union or the Jamaica Trades and Labour Union which, for the first time, was attempting to organise workers in the rural areas. However, within a year or two of its formation, this union was also defunct. DeLeon was also secretary of a committee formed by Marcus Garvey in 1930 'to pave the way for labour unions', which made representations to the Governor in support of a request for a minimum wage of a dollar (four shillings) a day.[19]

In February 1917 strikes occurred in the oilfields and at the Lake Asphalt Company in South Trinidad. Arising out of the latter strike, two of the strike leaders were sentenced to prison for two years and one to imprisonment for one year - all with hard labour. At around this time the trade unionist faction of the TWA, responding to the atmosphere of growing unrest among the workers, was taking steps to revive the organisation. By 1919 the TWA had adopted a policy of support for strikes and was endeavouring to negotiate wage increases. For the asphalt workers it negotiated a wage increase of thirty-three and a third percent and other appreciable benefits, which greatly increased its prestige.[20]

On 15 November 1919 the great strike of waterfront workers in Port of Spain commenced and the TWA was able to organise a massive popular demonstration in support which brought all business in the city to a stand-still. They negotiated a wage increase for the dock workers of twenty-five percent. But Braithwaite and other leaders of the TWA were sent to prison and the ageing DeBourg, despite his thirty years residence, was deported.[21] In 1917 there were strikes in St. Lucia following which merchants increased wages by fifteen percent and coal carriers received an increase of twenty-five percent. In Antigua there was a sugar workers strike in 1918 in which two workers were shot and killed.[22]

In 1917 the St. Kitts-Nevis Universal Benevolent Association was formed and registered as a Friendly Society. Some workers had wanted to form a trade union but because this would have been illegal the Friendly Societies Law was used. In 1918, following a sugar workers' strike, workers were imprisoned for breach of contract. The founders of this association were J. A. Nathan, a small shop-keeper who had become familiar with trade unions while residing in the USA, and J. M. Sebastian who started a newspaper called the *Union Messenger* in 1921.[23] No trade unions were formed in the Leeward or Windward Islands in the period following the First World War.

The first trade union enabling legislation was enacted in Jamaica in 1919, followed by British Guiana in 1921, but these statutes did not legalise peaceful picketing. This liberalism, if such it was, was not duplicated in Trinidad and Tobago where similar working class unrest to that which had resulted in the legalising of trade unions in Jamaica and British Guiana had occurred. Instead there was a spate of repressive legislation:

59

The Habitual Idlers Ordinance of 1918 was designed to discourage labourers whose terms of indenture had expired from leaving the plantations. It provided that any male who could not prove that he had worked for four hours per day during the preceding three days could be sent to a Government Labour Camp or contracted out by the Government to private employers.

The Strikes and Lockouts Ordinance of 1920, enacted immediately after the 1919 strikes and demonstrations, was a temporary measure which prohibited strikes and provided for arbitration to settle labour disputes. This was replaced by The Industrial Court Ordinance (No 26 of 1920) enacted in June 1920 which made some of the provisions of the temporary ordinance permanent.

The Seditious Acts and Publications Ordinance (No. 10 of 1920) banned a number of publications and created the offence of 'disaffection' against the King, the Government and the Executive and Legislative Councils, with penalties of up to two years imprisonment and/or a fine of up to £1,000.[24]

Trade union enabling legislation was not enacted in Trinidad and Tobago until 1932. Its passage was delayed pending the reference to the Colonial Office of the representations of the elected member Captain Arthur Cipriani that the Bill should be amended to include legalisation of peaceful picketing. At the same time similar legislation had been introduced in Grenada and T. A. Marryshow had secured an adjournment of the debate to await the decision on Cipriani's representations. When the Secretary of State rejected Cipriani's proposal the legislation was enacted in both colonies without a provision for peaceful picketing.

Not until 1939, after the major labour rebellions which occurred in the late 1930s and the hearings conducted by the West India Royal Commission in 1938 was legislation introduced in all the colonies which incorporated the right to conduct peaceful picketing and gave trade unions the same protection of their funds as existed in Britain.

Labour unrest in the post-World War I period appears to have developed somewhat later in Barbados than in the neighbouring islands, although there were demands for political reforms by the journalist C. W. Wickham. In 1924 Dr. C. Duncan O'Neale launched a political organisation called the Democratic

League. When the longshoremen went on strike in 1927, O'Neale volunteered his services to them and he subsequently formed the Workingmen's Association to act as a trade union bargaining agent.

In 1919 Captain Arthur Cipriani, a Trinidadian of Corsican descent who, as an officer of the West India Regiment, had established a reputation as the champion of the rights of the black soldiers serving in the First World War, returned to Trinidad. He was invited to and took over the Presidency of the TWA and under his charismatic leadership its membership rapidly increased. But Cipriani's orientation was political and, conscious of the fact that trade unions were still illegal, he discouraged the TWA from engaging in trade union activities. At the same time he agitated for a trade union law.

Several members of the TWA pressed for carrying on trade union activities regardless and this became a bone of contention in the organisation. Even when a trade union enabling ordinance was enacted in 1932, Cipriani was still opposed to the TWA engaging in trade union work because the Secretary of State had refused to incorporate a clause legalising peaceful picketing. Eventually, in 1934, he succeeded in having its name changed to the Trinidad Labour Party.

The third wave of labour unrest and organisation commenced in British Honduras in 1934. The outstanding leader to emerge there was Antonio Soberanis, a barber by trade who had lived in Central America and the USA In that year he formed the Labourers and Unemployed Association. There were widespread strikes and disturbances, but a trade union was not formally institutionalised until Soberanis and R. T. Meighan formed the British Honduras Workers' and Tradesmen's Union in 1939.

In the early 1930s a Workingmen's Association, patterned on the TWA, was formed in Grenada by T. A. Marryshow. In 1932 the St. Kitts Workers League was formed by Nathan and Sebastian. These were political organisations, not trade unions. In 1935 there was a general strike in St. Kitts. British warships were sent to the island and several strikers were killed. Not until 1940 was the St.Kitts-Nevis Trade & Labour Union founded, with Sebastian as President. Subsequently he was succeeded by Robert Bradshaw, a mechanic at the sugar factory who had been victimised.

In that same year there was labour unrest in St. Vincent which developed into a riot. The popular leader to emerge there was George McIntosh, owner of a small drug store. Arising out of these events McIntosh was charged with treason felony but the case was dismissed without the defence being called upon. In 1936 McIntosh organised the St. Vincent Workingmen's Cooperative Association which operated as a trade union despite the absence of enabling legislation.

There was a strike of coal heavers in St. Lucia in 1935 and the Governor summoned a British warship which played its searchlight on Castries, the capital, for several nights in a clear act of intimidation. A more extensive strike took place in 1937. In 1939 the first St. Lucian trade union was formed.

In March 1937 Clement Payne, born of Barbadian parents in Trinidad, came to Barbados. On 1 May of that year he commenced to organise the workers. Others who assisted him were Fitz Archibald Chase, Olrick Grant, Mortimer Skeete, Israel Lovell and Barnsley Alleyne. These were the pioneer labour leaders in Barbados during the third wave of labour unrest. The Governor's response was to deport Payne, which sparked off a riot in the course of which 14 were killed, 47 wounded and over 500 arrested. Grant and Skeete were sentenced to 10 years imprisonment, Lovell and Alleyne to 5 years each, Chase to nine months.[25]

In Trinidad, where there had been unemployed demonstrations in 1933 and 1934, a massive strike movement commenced and rioting occurred in 1937. A charismatic leader who emerged in the oilfields of South Trinidad was Tubal Uriah Butler, a migrant from Grenada. At the same time Adrian Cola Reinzi, a progressive lawyer who had been a sub-leader of the TWA and had broken with Cipriani in 1934 because of the latter's growing conservatism, assisted oilfield workers E. R. Blades, F. J. Rojas and Ralph Mentor in forming the Oilfield Workers Trade Union, and became its President.

Reinzi also assisted Macdonald Moses to form the All Trinidad Sugar Estates and Factory Workers Union. By the end of 1937 six trade unions had been registered and by the end of the following year the number had increased to ten. Other important leaders who were organising trade unions at this time were Rupert Gittens of the Public Works and Public Service

Union and Quintin O'Connor and Dudley Mahon of the Federated Workers Trade Union. O'Connor had formerly been Secretary of the Union of Shop Assistants, which merged with the FWTU when he became its Secretary. Clement Payne was one of the founders of the FWTU. Some of these new Unions formed the Committee of Industrial Organisations, which was the fore-runner of the Trade Union Council.

Butler had been imprisoned in September 1937. Released in May 1939, he was employed by the OWTU as an organiser. However Butler, a messianic leader, found difficulty in working in accordance with a committee's instructions. When an unauthorised strike occurred at the Lake Asphalt Company and the OWTU advised a return to work, Butler supported the strike. This led to his dismissal and he then formed his own organisation - the British Empire Workers and Citizens Home Rule Party.

In 1936 the Jamaica Workers and Tradesmen's Union, the first trade union of the third wave of working class unrest and organisation in the island, was organised by A. G. S. Coombs, an ex-soldier and policeman of peasant origin, and Hugh Clifford Buchanan, a master mason. The JWTU had a builders section led by Percy Aiken, veteran of the 1918 Railway strike, and C. W. Maxwell, a carpenter, but in 1938 this section hived off to become a Builders and Allied Workers Union.

The JWTU concentrated its organising efforts in the rural parishes. But this required transportation which they did not have, so they invited Alexander Bustamante, a public spirited money lender, to join them as Treasurer. This he did but he soon fell out with Coombs and left the JWTU. At the end of 1937 and beginning of 1938 Bustamante was offering himself in the role of a mediator between employers and employees.

In May 1938 there was a strike on the Kingston waterfront, and a strike of workers constructing a new sugar factory at the other end of the island which turned into a riot when an attempt was made to suppress it. The shippers rejected Bustamante's offer to mediate and the Governor ordered his imprisonment as an agitator, along with St. William Grant who had provided him with a platform for his public speeches. This was one of the sparks that ignited an all-island labour rebellion and brought almost all work to a stand-still.

Bustamante was released a week later and all charges against him were dropped. His release having been secured by the militancy of the workers, he emerged from custody no longer as a mediator but as a labour leader. He set about forming the Bustamante Industrial Trade Union, a blanket union organising all categories of workers of which Buchanan became the General Secretary. But Buchanan was also editor of the *Jamaica Labour Weekly* and in October 1938 he was imprisoned for six months for sedition.

The weapon of imprisonment was used quite extensively in Jamaica, not only against many striking workers but also against trade union leaders. In 1940 Bustamante, along with W. A. Williams, leader of the Kingston waterfront workers, was detained by the autocratic Governor without trial under war-time Defence Regulations. In 1942 Ken Hill, Secretary of the Postal and Telegraph Workers' Union, Frank Hill, President of the Public Works Employees' Union, Richard Hart, President of the Railway Employees' Union, and Arthur Henry, Secretary of the two last mentioned unions, were likewise detained without trial.

Among other trade union pioneers in Jamaica in the late 1930s and early 1940s were F. A. Glasspole, an accountant who became Secretary of the Jamaica United Clerks Association in 1937, Secretary of the Trade Union Council in 1939 and an officer of several other unions, and N. N. Nethersole, a solicitor, who became President of the TUC Ken Hill had been a Vice President of the BITU until 1939 and was also Secretary of the Tramway, Transport and General Workers Union, an officer of other unions and Vice President of the TUC.

In 1938 and 1939 there was labour unrest in British Guiana and many strikes occurred. Out of these there emerged a number of new trade unions and subsequently a Trade Union Council. A most important development in this period was the formation in November 1938 of the Man-Power Citizens Association, a trade union which, under the leadership of the jeweller Ayube Edun, organised sugar workers in British Guiana for the first time. The MPCA also organised bauxite workers. Between 1937 and 1938 seven new trade unions were formed. Among these were the Post Office Workers Union, the Transport and

Harbour Workers' Union, the Saw Mill Workers' Union and others. Meanwhile the BG Labour Union continued to function.

The third wave of unrest and organisation (1934-1942) in the English-speaking Caribbean region did not subside, as had been the case in the earlier waves of unrest and organisation. Instead it led to the formation of the permanent trade unions that we know today. However, with the passage of time, significant changes and developments would occur in the trade unions of the region.

In British Guiana the MPCA, which had pioneered the organisation of sugar plantation workers, underwent two significant changes. Firstly, the bauxite workers split off to form the BG Mineworkers Union. Secondly, the MPCA degenerated into a company union, which the plantation workers could no longer trust to represent them. Accordingly they transferred their allegiance to a new organisation, the Guyana Agricultural Workers' Union.[26]

In Jamaica, although during the pioneering period many separate industrial and occupational unions had come into existence along side, if not in harmony with, the BITU and had affiliated themselves to the Trade Union Council (TUC), these separate unions had in 1948 merged into one general or blanket union for which they retained the name Trade Union Congress. The only remaining difference between the two rival trade unions at that stage was that the TUC's leadership was democratically elected by the membership whereas, initially, the BITU's leadership was not.

Later, as a consequence of political developments in 1952, most of the members of the TUC transferred their membership to a new general workers union, the National Workers' Union. Later still another union, the University and Allied Workers' Union, developed into a general workers union which has attracted some members from both the BITU and NWU and from what remained of the TUC The vast majority of organised manual workers and many organised clerical workers in Jamaica are therefore now members of general workers unions although a few small separate unions still exist.

Subsequently the major unions, with the exception of the UAWU, and some of the smaller ones, agreed to come together to form a coordinating body. The main non-manual employees unions which are not affiliated are the Jamaica Teachers' Association (formerly the Jamaica Union of Teachers), the Civil Service Association and the Jamaica Association of Local Government Officers.

In Belize, Barbados, the Leeward Islands and the Windward Islands, mainly because of their smaller populations or size, the general workers union has always been the main organisational pattern. Only in Trinidad and Tobago and Guyana are industrial unions the main form of trade union organisation.

Chapter 7

The Political Awakening

The Crown Colony system had been introduced first in Trinidad and St. Lucia when the British Government acquired these colonies. It had been adopted in all the older internally self-governing colonies except Barbados and the Bahamas following the Morant Bay Rebellion in Jamaica in 1865. It had also been duplicated in the mainland colonies of British Guiana and British Honduras. This system had vested almost complete political control of these colonies in the British Government.

In 1874 the Jamaica Association, formed in that year, advocated the admission into the Legislative Council, then consisting entirely of Government officials, of unofficial members to be nominated by the Governor and members to be elected by persons who paid one pound annually in direct taxes. When however their petition, signed by 2,447 persons, was presented in 1876, the request for inclusion of elected members was omitted. In 1883 a somewhat bolder petition, signed by 4,677 persons including Custodes, magistrates, solicitors, clergymen and representatives of commercial firms, asked for a Legislative Council of 8 nominated and 14 elected members.[1]

In 1884, in response to this petition the Secretary of State for the Colonies agreed to a Legislative Council for Jamaica consisting of the Governor, the Officer commanding British troops on the island, three ex-officio Civil Servants, not exceeding 5 persons to be nominated by the British Government and 9 elected members. The right to vote was then restricted to males possessing an annual income of £150 from land or £200 partly from land and partly from an office or business, or £300 from an office or business provided that such voters had paid annual direct taxes or customs duties of not less than £10.[2] In 1895, in response to a further petition, the number of elected members was increased to 14, but the number of ex-officio members was increased to 5 and authority was given to the Governor to appoint up to 10 nominated members.

Many attempts were made to arouse nationalistic sentiments and create a demand for democratic rights and petitions for constitutional reforms were sent to Britain from several colonies. In 1881 there was a petition from Grenada. There, in 1883 the first demand for the right to be represented by non-Whites was articulated by William Galway Donovan, the proprietor and editor of a newspaper called the *Grenada People*. He and eighteen others submitted a memorandum to the West Indies Royal Commission of that year, complaining that the denial of a right to elect representatives was a racist attitude.

Imprisoned for libel Donovan responded defiantly:

> I shall continue in my journal to advocate the right of the people of Grenada to representative government ... believing as I do that the people of the colony are qualified to manage through their representatives all local affairs and that until this fundamental right is restored ... neither the prosperity of the colony nor the contentment of the people will be ensured.[3]

In Jamaica in 1885 Dr Robert Love, an advocate of the right of all adult Jamaicans to vote and be elected to public office, had started a newspaper called the *Jamaica Advocate*. In this paper he endeavoured to develop racial pride in a mainly black population that had been successfully indoctrinated with the belief that black people were inferior to whites. In 1889, having been elected to the Kingston Municipal Council in the previous year, he established a political organisation called the People's Convention.

In 1881, when the total population of Jamaica was 580,804,[4] the number of registered voters was 7,443. 1001 of these were white, 2578 were mulatto (of mixed European and African descent – hereinafter referred to as 'brown'), 3766 were black and 98 were Indian. Love disclosed that many black and brown men who had the necessary qualifications had not registered themselves as electors. He therefore led a campaign to encourage people to register. As a result, by 1899 the number of registered voters had increased to 42,266. This so alarmed the Governor and the white plantation owners that a literacy test was introduced. As a result of this the number of registered voters was reduced by approximately half.

Initially the political institutions in British Guiana had been quite different to those in place in the other British colonies in the Caribbean region. This had been because the colony consisted of an amalgamation of the three former Dutch colonies of Essequibo, Berbice and Demerara which had been occupied by Britain in 1803-4 and formally ceded to Britain in 1814.

In 1887 the British Guiana Reform Club was formed. Although its membership was not very broad, it organised a demand for representative government which was signed by 4,647 Guianese. The term 'representative government' meant that there should be a majority of elected members in the legislature. In August 1889 the British Guiana Constitutional Reform Association was founded by R. P. Drysdale, who was then Mayor of Georgetown and what was known as a 'Financial Representative' on the 'Combined Court'. But in 1890 the coloured barrister Duncan Hudson, who was the Association's first candidate to be elected as a Financial Representative, was defeated by the candidate of the sugar plantation interests.

Constitutional amendments were introduced in British Guiana in 1890 but, as the *Berbice Gazette* of 29 November commented, these were:

> so slight ... that it is hardly worth while making them at all. The number of the Court of Policy ... is to be increased [to 16 – eight officials and eight elected members] but the qualifications being the possession of property of large value, there will be practically no difference in the class of persons eligible for the Legislature, as comparatively few persons unconnected with the planting industry hold property to the value of $7,500.

The number of eligible voters in the general election held in British Guiana in 1892 was only 2,046. In the newly elected Combined Court, in which the number of elected members had been increased to 14, 12 were white. The Court of Policy consisted of 5 white planters, 2 white merchants and one coloured barrister.

The Trinidad Workingmen's Association was formed in 1897, performing the functions of both an illegal trade union seeking wage increases and a political pressure group. Giving evidence before the West Indies Royal Commission in that year its President Walter Mills outlined a number of proposals and complaints and said:

we shall always suffer these injustices as long as we have not the right of sending our representatives to the Legislative Council...

By the end of the century Representative Government Associations had also been formed in the smaller islands of St. Kitts, St. Lucia and Dominica.

In the early 1890s there were still no black members of the Legislative Council in Jamaica although a few blacks had been elected to the Local Authorities then known as Parochial Boards. In 1893 four brown men were elected to the Legislative Council.[5] In a general election held in 1889 Alexander Dixon was the first black man to be elected to the Legislative Council.

In 1895 the number of elected representative in the Jamaican legislature was increased to 14, one for each of the island's 14 parishes. At that time the right to vote was confined to male property owners and tax-payers and the great majority of the adult male population was disfranchised. When female voters first acquired the right to vote in 1919, they had to be not less than 25 years of age (as against 21 years of age for men) and their land tax qualification was an annual payment of £2 (as compared to ten shillings per year for men).

Dr Love was elected to the Legislative Council in 1906. He was a member of Jamaica's first nationalistic political organisation – the National Club. This had been formed in 1909 and was led by S. A. G. (Sandy) Cox. In its manifesto the National Club declared:

> Each member pledges himself to do all he can to secure self government for this island. Its founders expressed their intention to correct abuses by the Government and to put themselves in communication with those Trade Unions in England (and if possible to affiliate with them) as also Labour members of Parliament.

Cox also founded and edited a newspaper called *Our Own*. In the issue of this paper published on 15 August 1910 he wrote 'We desire a greater measure of self government within the Empire'.

Although the National Club was a political organisation, it was not a political party in the modern sense of that term. It did not seek to have a mass membership or branch structure and was little more than an association of persons with ad-

70

vanced political ideas, most of whom aspired to be elected to the legislature. It did however have as its secretaries two young men who would play an important part in future developments – Marcus Garvey and W. A. Domingo.

In a general election held in 1911 three of the National Club's candidates, Dixon, Cox and another, were elected. Cox however lost his seat as a result of an election petition because he was unable to prove that he resided within his constituency, a requirement at that time. Disappointed and disillusioned, he emigrated to the United States of America and the National Club soon ceased to function. Love died in 1914.

In 1921 the British Government appointed E. F. L. Wood to review and report on constitutional government in the British West Indies. He visited most of the colonies and reported his recommendations in the course of the following years. He recommended the merger of Tobago with Trinidad and the creation of a Legislative Council to consist of the Governor with an original and casting vote, 12 government officials, 6 unofficial members appointed by the Governor and 7 elected members one of whom would be for Tobago. Candidates for election were to be males literate in English, who owned real estate worth not less than TT$1,920 or had an annual income exclusively from land of not less than TT$960 or from other sources of TT$1,920.

Recommendations as to the right to vote were complicated. It was to be restricted to males over 21 years of age and females over 30 years of age who possessed one of the following qualifications - ownership of property of a rateable value of TT$60 in a borough or TT$48 elsewhere; payment of a rental of TT$60 in a borough or TT$48 elsewhere or rent and board of combined of TT$300; payment of annual land taxes of TT$2.40; receipt of an annual salary of not less than TT$300.[6] His recommendations were accepted by the British Government and introduced in 1925.

A general election held in British Guiana in 1926 resulted in several seats being won by the new Popular Party headed by Nelson Cannon and the popular coloured journalist A.R.F. Webber. This had worried plantation owners. Commissioners sent by the British Government to report on the affairs of the colony recommended constitutional changes which were introduced in Parliament by the British Guiana Act of 1928. This legislation replaced the Combined Court and the Court of Policy, which had been inherited from the Dutch, by a Legislative Council consisting of the Governor, ten Government officials, five unofficial members nominated by the Governor and 14 elected members. The Governor was given power to approve any measure defeated in the Legislative Council which he considered necessary.

In 1924 Duncan O'Neal, a physician who had been a member of the socialist Fabian Society in Britain, return to Barbados. He founded the Democratic League. At that time voters in Barbados were required to have either an annual income of not less than £50 or to own land of a rental value of not less than £5 per year. In December of that year the League's candidate C. A. Braithwaite won a seat in the Barbados Assembly in a by-election.

In 1928 Marcus Garvey, now internationally famous as the leader of the Universal Negro Improvement Association, was released from prison in the USA and deported to Jamaica. He put together a group of candidates under the name 'Peoples Political Party' to contest a general election in 1930, but due to the restricted franchise Garvey and all but one of its ten candidates were defeated. Nothing more was heard of this organisation after the election. Garvey however won a seat on the Kingston and St. Andrew municipal council.

The numbers of voters in the 1930s and their percentages of the population they comprised were as follows:[7]

Colony	No. of Electors	Population Percentage
Antigua	1,048	3.06
Barbados	6,359	3.30
Br. Guiana	9,578	2.84
Br. Honduras	1,156	2.00
Dominica	1,248	2.46
Grenada (1921)	-	2.46
Jamaica	61,621	5.25
Montserrat	260	1.90
St. Kitts	1,628	2.30
St. Lucia	1,509	2.18
St. Vincent	1,598	2.78
Trinidad-Tobago	30,911	6.64
Bahamas	13,146	21.97

All this was to change as a result of popular political awakening that occurred in parallel with the wave of working class unrest and organisation that swept across the English speaking Caribbean region in the 1930s.[8]

Chapter 8

Foundations of Independence

The British Government did not willingly surrender its sovereignty over its North American colonies. British military forces sent to suppress the rebellious Americans had only abandoned that task and withdrawn when it was recognised that defeat was inevitable. Thereafter the British Government had acquiesced in Australia, New Zealand and South Africa, colonies inhabited by Whites or (in the case of South Africa) controlled by the white inhabitants, becoming politically independent 'dominions'. The relationship between Britain and these territories would thereafter be known as the 'British Commonwealth', to distinguish it from Britain's continuing relationship with her non-self governing colonies.

Although, as we have seen, demands for democratic reforms were being made in many of the remaining colonies, the British imperialists had not anticipated that a similar transition to political independence would occur in what remained of the British Empire. Demands for constitutional reform were however increasing, not only in the West Indian colonies but also, and perhaps more importantly, in India and Burma.

When the British Government appointed a Royal Commission in 1938, it had hoped to exclude constitutional issues from its investigations and recommendations. It was appointed:

> To investigate social and economic conditions in Barbados, British Guiana, British Honduras, Jamaica, the Leeward Islands, Trinidad & Tobago, and the Windward Islands and matters connected therewith and to make recommendations.[1]

As this limitation of its functions had led to criticisms, the Secretary of State for the Colonies had made a tactical retreat. On the eve of its departure for Jamaica, its first port of call, he had sent a telegram to the Officer Administering the Government:

> commission may also wish to hear evidence about the Jamaica constitution and organisation of local government so

far as may be necessary to elucidate social and economic problems.[2]

The Commission did hear evidence on constitutional questions but in its report it said:

> We do not support ... the extreme proposals put before us for the grant of immediate and complete self-government based on universal suffrage ... because it would render impossible the financial control necessary if, as we consider to be inevitable, substantial assistance is to be afforded by His Majesty's Government through the West Indian Welfare Fund. ... At the present stage, we attach more importance to the truly representative character of Legislative Councils than to any drastic change in their functions.[3]

Events were also influenced by the outbreak of the Second World War in 1939 and the initial victories of Germany in Europe and Japan in the east.

The formation of political parties, in anticipation of the achievement of political independence, began in Jamaica in 1938 with the founding of the People's National Party, led by the barrister Norman Manley. The Jamaica Labour Party, led by W. A. Bustamante, was launched in 1943. In 1944 a Political Action Committee was formed in British Guiana, to lay the foundations for a political party. In 1950 the People's Progressive Party, built on the same lines as the Jamaican People's National Party, was launched. Unlike earlier political groups in the British Caribbean region colonies, the PNP and the PPP were real political parties with local branches and mass memberships. Organisations with the objective of achieving political independence were also launched in other Caribbean area colonies.

In the 1940s the Government of the United States of America was becoming increasingly concerned about the growing unrest in Caribbean territories on its door-step. Britain, which was becoming increasingly dependent on the USA for military supplies and in other respects, was no longer able to ignore American concerns.

On 14 August 1941 a meeting took place on a warship in mid-Atlantic between US President Franklin Roosevelt and British Prime Minister Winston Churchill. While the USA was still nominally neutral, Roosevelt was preparing his nation for entry into the war and the two leaders drew up a joint declaration, to become known as the 'Atlantic Charter'. In this they set out their war aims and their ideas for a post-war world. The third clause of the document read:

> They respect the right of all peoples to choose the form of government under which they will live; and they wish to see sovereign rights and self government restored to all those who have been forcibly deprived of them.[4]

There was no doubt in Roosevelt's mind that these words were of general application. But no sooner had Churchill returned to England than he declared that they were only meant to apply to countries occupied by the enemy and did not apply to the British Empire. Not surprisingly, there was an immediate protest from many British colonies. Roosevelt too was reported to have been annoyed, but refrained from issuing a contradiction.

Responding to enquiries from India, Burma, West Africa and Ceylon as to the application of the Charter, Churchill made a statement in the House of Commons on 9 September 1941 in which he made reference to:

> the statements of policy ... made from time to time about the development of constitutional government in India, Burma and other parts of the British Empire ... We had in mind, primarily, the restoration of the sovereignty ... of the states and nations of Europe now under Nazi yoke ... that is a separate problem from the evolution of self governing institutions in ... regions and peoples which owe allegiance to the British Crown. We have made declarations on these matters which are ... free from ambiguity and related to the ... territories and peoples affected...

When however Creech-Jones, a Labour Party member, asked: 'will the Right Honourable Gentleman publish those declarations?' Churchill could make no reply. No such declarations had ever been made.

On 27 October 1942 *The Times* published a report of a meeting between US President Franklin D. Roosevelt and Sir William Gater, the British Under Secretary of State sent to the USA at President Roosevelt's request to discuss American concerns. The President was reported to have told the British diplomat that he thought that there should be:

an extension of the franchise, in compulsory education and in an attempt to make the islands self-sustaining ... He hoped for a new economic social system ... a big improvement on present conditions...

The report said further that 'Asked if it would require some form of political unity' the President had replied: 'Certainly not, but it would require more self-government'.[5]

In 1944 the British Government agreed to introduce full adult suffrage in Jamaica and a new constitution which, though still far short of political independence, was a step in that direction. In 1947, faced with the inevitable, it conceded political independence to India. This was to turn out to be the beginning of the eventual end of Empire.

In 1948 the Trinidad & Tobago Legislative Council was allowed to appoint a committee to draw up proposals for a new constitution, which was introduced there in 1950. It seems improbable that at that time the British Government had intended to concede, to even its larger Caribbean region colonies, more than a right to control their internal affairs. However, the combination of the determination of West Indian peoples to achieve political independence and American pressure upon Britain to decolonise proved irresistible.

At a conference held in London in April 1953, representatives of the British colonies in the Caribbean islands had agreed to a proposal that their countries should participate in a Federation. The legislatures of the two mainland colonies of British Guiana and British Honduras had however decided not to participate.

As the islands had been federated with their existing colonial constitutions, several colonies had pursued parallel negotiations with the British Government with a view to upgrading their insular constitutions to the level of control of their own internal affairs, then referred to as 'internal self-government'. As a result of such negotiations, improvements of some insular constitutions had been obtained. Although the constitution fell far short of political independence, Article 118 of the Federal Constitution had provided that:

> Not later than the fifth anniversary of the date on which this Constitution comes into force there shall be a conference

convened consisting of the delegates from the Federation, from each of the Colonies referred to in paragraph (1) of article 1 of this Constitution and from the United Kingdom chosen by their respective Governments, for the purpose of reviewing this Constitution.

It was generally believed at the time that this meant that at such a conference it would be possible to negotiate the achievement of 'dominion status' for the Federation. However in April 1958 Ken Hill, who had joined the Jamaica Labour Party and been elected to the Federal Parliament, proposed a Motion calling for the appointment of a Joint Committee to formulate proposals for Dominion Status for the Federation 'at the earliest date'.

According to John Mordecai, the Federal Secretary (later to become the Federation's Deputy Governor General), this was a 'strategic move', approved in advance by Bustamante and other JLP leaders, 'to claim credit for initiating a more rapid achievement of Dominion Status' for the Federation. The Federal Government endeavoured to counter this move by proposing that Hill's resolution be amended to read: 'that the conference envisaged by Article 118 be convened not later than June 1959, to prepare for the achievement of Dominion status within the Commonwealth at the earliest possible moment'. This amendment was approved.

All these manoeuvres were however soon proved to be irrelevant when, in a referendum held on 19 September 1961 to answer the question 'Should Jamaica remain in the Federation of the West Indies', the Jamaican electorate, rejecting Premier Norman Manley's advice, decided that it should not. Of the 777,965 persons eligible to vote, 479,220 or 61.6 per cent had voted. This compared with just over 66 per cent of the eligible voters who had voted in the 1959 general election. Of the 477,580 valid votes cast just over 54 per cent had voted for Jamaica to leave the Federation while just under 46 percent had voted for Jamaica to stay in. The majority for leaving the Federation was 38,942. The Jamaican vote effectively spelled the death of the Federation. Attempts to reconstruct a Federation without Jamaica soon collapsed.

The British Government conceded political independence to Jamaica in 1962. It also recognised that, having allowed Jamaica to proceed to separate independence, it could not resist a similar demand from Trinidad & Tobago and later in the same year it conceded independence there.

A conference to consider a demand for constitutional advancement for British Guiana, which was not part of the West Indian Federation, had been held in London in March 1960, chaired by the Secretary of State for the Colonies. At that conference it had been agreed that internal self government would be introduced in 1961. It had also been agreed that one year after a general election to be held in 1961 or on the achievement of independence by the West Indies Federation, which ever might be earlier, a conference would be held to consider the terms on which British Guiana would become independent.

The Government of the USA however saw things different-ly. At talks held in Washington in February 1961 between representatives of the British and American Governments, Bill Burdet, Director of the US Office of British Commonwealth and Northern European Affairs, had asked the British representative if something could be done to 'ensure that someone other than the PPP won the August elections'. If not, whether independence could be delayed as a means of buying time while alternative 'democratic' forces were matured.[6]

The British Prime Minister was uneasy about the leftist nature of the Peoples Progressive Party. He however felt that, in view of the commitment that had been made, there was no viable alternative to continuing to work with Cheddi Jagan and to concede independence to British Guiana too in 1962. The Amer-icans however saw things differently. After the PPP had won the general election held in August 1961, they stepped up their intervention in the affairs of British Guiana. Arthur Schlesinger, adviser to US President Kennedy, gave this description of US Government policy:

> The idea, in short, is to use the year or two before independ-ence to work to tie Jagan to the political and economic framework of the hemisphere, while at the same time rein-suring against pro-Communist developments by building anti-Communist clandestine capabilities [and to] develop information about, expose and destroy Communists in Brit-ish Guiana, including, if necessary, the possibility of finding a substitute for Jagan himself.

Schlesinger did not specify the form that these 'clandestine capabilities' were to take, but in a memorandum on the following day he said that the 'first emphasis' was to be on 'intelligence collection, with covert political action to come later'.[7]

In February 1962 US Secretary of State Dean Rusk wrote this brusque letter to Lord Home, the British Foreign Secretary:

> You know from our correspondence in August of last year of my acute concern over the prospects of an independent British Guiana under the leadership of Cheddi Jagan. Subsequently to his victory in the August elections we agreed to try your policy of fostering an effective association between British Guiana and the West...
>
> In pursuance of the program the President received Jagan on his visit to this country in October. I must tell you now that I have reached the conclusion that it is not possible for us to put up with an independent British Guiana under Jagan...

Not surprisingly, British Prime Minister Macmillan was offended by the tone of the American's letter and he expressed this in a Minute to the Foreign Secretary. In reply to Rusk he wrote:

> You say that it is not possible for you 'to put up with an independent British Guiana under Jagan' and that 'Jagan should not accede to power again'. How would you suggest that this can be done in a democracy ? And even if a device could be found, it would almost certainly be transparent ... So I would say to you that we cannot now go back on the course we have set ourselves of bringing these dependent territories to self-government. Nor is it any good deluding ourselves that we can now set aside a single territory such as British Guiana for some sort of special treatment.[8]

However, despite these initial protests, the British Government did cave in to American pressure and find a way of getting Jagan and the PPP out of office. This was done by changing the long standing British 'first past the post' electoral system to a system known as 'Proportional Representation'. This facilitated the defeat of the PPP in a general election held in December 1964. In that election the seats obtained by two opposition parties, the People's National Congress led by L. F. S. Burnham and the so-called United Force led by Peter D'Aguiar, exceeded the number of seats won by the PPP. The PPP won 24 seats, the PNC 22 and the UF 7 seats.

In 1966, the PPP having been removed from office, independence was conceded to a British Guiana led by Burnham. In that same year independence was conceded to Barbados. Having relinquished control of its principal colonies in the Caribbean area, the British Government appears to have come to the conclusion that it might as well allow its remaining colonies to secede if they wished to do so.

The first of these colonies to opt for independence was Grenada, which became independent in 1974. The last to go, in 1981, were St. Kitts-Nevis and British Honduras. All that then remained in the Caribbean of the once proud British Empire was Montserrat, the British Virgin Islands and Anguilla. These tiny islands, of no economic or political value to the metropolis, decided to retain their colonial status.

Endnotes

Introduction

1. C. L. R. James, "The Making of the Caribbean People" in *Spheres of Existence: Selected Writings*, Allison and Busby, London, 1966; 1980, p. 173. See also Anthony Bogues, *Caliban's Freedom: The Early Political Thought of C. L. R. James*, Pluto Press, London, 1997, pp. 23-24 for a critical comment on this aspect of James's thought.
2. Eric Williams, *Capitalism and Slavery*, Andre Deutsch, London, 1964.
3. Frantz Fanon, *Peau noire, masques blancs*, Editions du Seuil, Paris, 1952; *Black Skin, White Masks*, trans. Charles Lam Markmann, Grove Press, New York 1965.
4. George Beckford, *Persistent Poverty: Underdevelopment in Plantation Economies of the Third World*, Oxford University Press, London, 1972.
5. Walter Rodney, *How Europe Underdeveloped Africa*, Bogle-L'Ouverture, London, 1972.
6. Joy DeGruy-Leary, *Post Traumatic Slave Syndrome – America's Legacy to Enduring Injury and Healing*, Uptone Press, Oregon, 2005.
7. C. L. R. James, op. cit., p. 176.
8. See, for example, Fidel Castro, with Ignacio Ramonet, *My Life*, Penguin Books, Harmondsworth, 2008, pp. 308-334; and *passim* and Walter Rodney, 'Support for Liberation Struggles in Southern Africa', Text of an address made to the Afro-Asian Cultural Society, Sussex University, 1977. (Reprinted by the Walter Rodney Memorial Committee and the Working People's Alliance Support Group, London. Reprinted by the Working People's Alliance, Guyana on the occasion of African Liberation Day, 1987).

Chapter 2

1. The term 'indentured' was derived from the practice that contracts had originally been handwritten on parchment in duplicate, the duplicates being side by side. These were then cut apart not in a straight line but in an indented manner and one copy was held by each party. It was then possible, by fitting the two parts together, to ensure that both were genuine.
2. P. D. Curtin, *The Atlantic Slave Trade: A Census*, Wisconsin University Press, Madison WI, 1969, pp. 34, 46.

3. DeCastro e Almeida, *Conquests And Discoveries Of Henry The Navigator*, Allen & Unwin, London, 1936, Chap. 1.
4. Noël Deerr, *The History of Sugar*, (2 vols.) Chapman and Hall, London, 1949/50, vol. 2, p. 284.
5. Richard Hakluyt (ed.), *The Principal Navigations, Voyages, Traffiques and Discoveries of the English Nation*, London 1589 (reprinted J. M. Dent, London & Toronto, 1927).
6. Stanlake Samkange, 'Wars of resistance' in A. M. Josephy (ed.) *The Horizon History Of Africa*, American Heritage Publishing Co., New York, 1971.
7. Eric Williams, 'The Golden Age of the Slave System in Britain' in *Journal of Negro History*, Vol. 25, No. 1 (January 1940).
8. W. W. Claridge, *A History of the Gold Coast and Ashanti*, John Murray, London, 1915, Vol. 1, p.173. Claridge's source, not given, was probably Henry Barth, *Travels And Discoveries in Northern and Central Africa*, London (2nd ed., 1857) who accompanied the Bornu army in its expedition against Musgu in 1795-97.
9. B. Martin and M. Spurell (eds), *Journal Of A Slave Trader*, Epworth Press, London, 1962, p.109.
10. D. B. Davis, *The Problem of Slavery in Western Culture*, Penguin Books, London, 1970, p. 294.
11. G. F. Dow, *Slave Ships And Slaving*, Marine Research Society, Salem, USA, 1927, p. 68.
12. Martin and Spurell, op. cit., p. 81n.
13. C. S. Higham, *The Development Of The Leeward Islands Under The Restoration 1660-1688*, Cambridge, 1921, p. 158.
14. Curtin, op. cit., p. 151.
15. G. Martin, *Nantes au XVIII Siècle: L'Ere des Negrières 1714-1744*, Paris, 1931 cited in Curtin, op. cit.
16. D. P. Mannix and M. Cowley, *Black Cargoes: A History of the Atlantic Slave Trade 1518 to 1865*, Viking Press, New York, 1962.

Chapter 3

1. Karl Marx, *Capital. Vol. 1*, Charles H. Kerr & Co., Chicago, 1906, p. 293.
2. *Parliamentary Accounts And Papers, 1790-1*, Vol. 92.
3. Such legislation, though not very effective, was enacted in Jamaica in 1751, 1779, 1782, 1788, 1792 and 1800. See Orlando Patterson, *The Sociology of Slavery*, MacGibbon & Kee, London, 1967, pp. 73-9.

4. John Newton, *Thoughts Upon The African Slave Trade*, London, 1788, reprinted in Martin and Spurell, op. cit.

5. *Jamaica Assembly Votes*, 18 November, 1831.

6. W. J. Gardner, *The History of Jamaica*, (1st edition 1873), T. Fisher Unwin, London, 1909, pp. 244-5.

7. Alan Burns, *History of the British West Indies*, Allen & Unwin, London, 1954, p. 629, quoting Statement No. 93 printed 9 March, 1838 by order of the House of Commons.

8. Edward Long, *The History of Jamaica*, (2 vols.) London, 1774; vol. 2, pp. 351-6, 365, 370-1, 374-7.

9. Tharp Papers, Cambridgeshire Record Office, R55.7.123/11.

Chapter 4

1. William Snelgrave, *New Account of Guinea*, London, 1734, p.173.

2. Dow, op. cit., pp. 65-67.

3. Goulburn Papers, Surrey Record Office: Alex Moir to Mrs Mumbee Goulburn, 10 April,

1 May and 15 May, Mrs Goulburn to Thomas Samson, Overseer, 7 August 1802.

4. R. Hart, *Slaves Who Abolished Slavery*, vol. 2: *Blacks in Rebellion*, University of the West Indies Press, Kingston, 2002; R. Hart, *The Abolition of Slavery*, Community Education Trust, London, 1988; L. Honychurch, *The Dominica Story*, Macmillan, London, 1995.

5. C. L. R. James, *The Black Jacobins*, (2nd ed.) Knopf and Random House, New York, 1963.

6. R. Hart, *Slaves Who Abolished Slavery*, vol. 1: *Blacks in Bondage*, Institute of Social & Economic Studies, Kingston, 1980, pp. 152-66.

7. *Parliamentary Debates* (2nd Series) IX, 285-6.

8. R. Hart, *Slaves Who Abolished Slavery*, vol. 1. p. 220: Resolution of the Anti-Slavery Society, London, May 1830.

9. Honychurch, op. cit., pp.111-14.

10. R. Hart, *Slaves Who Abolished Slavery*, vol. 2, pp. 225-7.

11. Hilary Beckles, *Black Rebellion in Barbados*, Antilles Publications, Bridgetown, 1984.

12. Mary Turner, Slaves and Missionaries, Kingston, University of the West Indies Press, Kingston, 1982 citing 'Report of the Proceedings against ... Rev. J. Smith' by the London Missionary Society, and articles in *Weslyan-Methodist Magazine*, January, 1824.

13. *Parliamentary Accounts and Papers*, Vol. XVII, pp. 219-25.

14. Henry Bleby, *Death Struggles of Slavery* (3rd ed.), London, 1868, pp. 25-30.

15. Ibid., p. 117. Bleby had been smeared with tar by the members of the Colonial Church Union who attacked him and was only saved from being burned alive by the timely arrival of his wife and supporters.

16. M. Reckord, 'The Jamaica Slave Rebellion of 1831', *Past and Present*, No. 40, July, 1968.

17. H. M. Waddell, *Twenty-Nine Years in the West Indies and Central Africa*, London, 1863, pp. 55-6.

18. Ibid., p. 51.

19. Bleby, op. cit., p. 118.

Chapter 5

1. Ansell Hart, *The Life Of George William Gordon*, Institute of Jamaica, n.d., pp. 23, 27.

2. Gad Heuman, *The Killing Time: The Morant Bay Rebellion in Jamaica*, Macmillan, London, 1994, pp. 57-9.

3. Ansell Hart, op. cit. pp. 44-51 and 61-7, quoting Underhill to Cardwell, 5 January, and Cardwell to Eyre 14 June 1865.

4. Ibid., p. 75.

5. Richard Hart, *From Occupation to Independence: A Short History of the Peoples of the English-Speaking Caribbean Region*, Pluto Press, London, 1998, Chap. 13. Whether the release of the prisoners from the gaol took place before or after the events at the Court House is not clear.

6. Gad Heuman, op. cit., p. 22.

7. Ibid., pp. 17-28.

8. Ibid., citing Public Record Office 884/2 – Confidential Print No. 2 – 'Papers Relating to the Insurrection in Jamaica, Printed for the Use of the Cabinet, December 1865', p. 23.

9. Ansell Hart, op. cit. pp. 86-7, quoting Lord Olivier, *The Myth of Governor Eyre*, Hogarth Press, London, 1933.

10. Ansell Hart, op. cit. pp. 91-2.

11. Gad Heuman, op. cit. pp. 87-91 and 139.

12. *The Laws of Jamaica* (1865), Cap. XXIV, 'An Act to Amend an Act passed in the present Session'.

Chapter 6

1. *Laws of Jamaica*, 1839 Chap. XXX; R. Gonsalves, 'The Trade Union Movement in Jamaica' in C. Stone & A. Brown (eds), *Essays in Power and Change in Jamaica*, Publishing House, Kingston, Ja. 1977, p. 9.

2. J. R. Green, *A Short History of the English People*, London, J. M. Dent, 1915, p.824

3. Public Record Office: CO 137/674 - Memo initialled by G. G. endorsed on Olivier's despatch No. 518 dated 20 November 1909. The writer is indebted to Dr. Richard Lobdell for identifying its author as G. Grindle, senior adviser and later private secretary to the Permanent Under Secretary for Colonial Affairs. Grindle was later appointed Governor of the Windward Islands.

4. G. Eaton, 'Trade Union Development in Jamaica' in *Caribbean Quarterly*, Vol.8, Nos. 1 & 2.

5. *Daily Gleaner*, 31 March, 1994 - 'The J.U.T./J.T.A. in Trade Union Perspective'

6. Interview by A. J. McGlashan with Richard Hart, 7 & 10 February, 1958.

7. Ibid.

8. *Daily Gleaner*, 17 April 1919, cited in Eaton, op. cit.

9. Walter Rodney, *A History of the Guyanese Working People 1881-1905*, Heinemann, London, 1981, pp. 104, 154, 157-8, 163-5, 191, 209-10.

10. Ashton Chase, *A History of Trade Unionism in Guyana 1900-1961*, New Guyana Co., Georgetown, 1964 pp. 25-6.

11. Nigel Boland, *On The March: Labour Rebellions in the British Caribbean 1934-1939*, Ian Randle, Kingston, 1995, pp. 7-12.

12. Chase, op. cit., pp. 51-72.

13. Recollections of Edward Reid to the writer, c. 1950.

14. R. A. Lobdell, Jamaican Labor, 1838-1938, University of Wisconsin, Madison, 1968, citing *Daily Chronicle*, 12 October 1917.

15. *Jamaica Times*, 20 October 1917.

16. Interview of Percy A. Aiken with Richard Hart, 14 November 1950.

17. Lobdell, op. cit., citing *Daily Gleaner*, 27 June and 23 August, 1919; interview with A. J. McGlashan.

18. Eaton, op. cit., p. 45.

19. *Daily Gleaner*, 13 May 1930.

20. *The Blackman* [Garvey's paper], 12 April 1930.

21. Selwyn Ryan, 'Rise and Fall of the Barefooted Man' in *Trinidad & Tobago Index*, Winter 1966, No. 3, pp. 5, 24.

22. Jos. N. France, *Working Class Struggles of Half a Century* (an unpublished manuscript of a collection of articles by this author for the *Union Messenger*).

23. Keith Hunte, 'Duncan O'Neale, the Apostle of Freedom' in *New World Quarterly*, Vol. 3, Nos.1 & 2 (1966), p. 85,

24. Wendy Charles, *Early Labour Organisation in Trinidad and the Colonial Context of the Butler Riots*, Dept. of Sociology, University of the West Indies, St. Augustine, 1978 pp.10-12.

25. F. Mark, *The History Of The Barbados Workers Union*, Bridgetown, Barbados, nd. pp. 1-5; Hilary Beckles, *A History Of Barbados*, Cambridge University. Press, 1990; Hunte, op. cit., p.85.

26. Chase, op. cit.

Chapter 7

1. *Petition from the Inhabitants of Jamaica ... together with the Reply of Her Majesty's Government...*, Eyre & Spottiswoode, London, 1884, presented to both Houses of Parliament.

2. Order in Council, 19 May, 1884. (Jamaica Archives 21/300).

3. George Brizan, *Grenada, Island of Conflict*, London, Zed Books, 1984, citing Report of the Royal Commission, Part 2, p. 58 and the *St. Georges Chronicle & Grenada Gazette*, 9 May, 1885.

4. *Eighth Census of Jamaica*, Government Printer, Kingston, 1943.

5. Philip Sherlock and Hazel Bennett, *The Story of the Jamaican People*, Ian Randle, Kingston, 1998.

6. Eric Williams, *History of the People of Trinidad & Tobago*, Andre Deutsch, London, 1964, pp. 219-20.

7. Public Record Office, London CO 318/436/6 and File 71013 – Electors of the West Indies (1938)

8. Williams, op. cit., pp. 219-20.

Chapter 8

1. *West India Royal Commission Report*, HM Stationery Office, London, 1945, p. xiii.

2. Public Record Office: CO 318/434/8 File 71175 – telegram 8 August 1938.

3. *West India Royal Commission Report*.

4. G. M. Howat (ed.), *Dictionary of World History*, Nelson, London, 1973, pp. 110-11.

5. Public Record Office: CO 318/452 File 71265, CO 318/455//2 File 71307 and CO 318/455/6 File 71317

6. Record of Anglo-US talks, 9 February 1961 – Ref. ZP 14/39G and Public Record Office, London, FO 371/159672, cited in the Ph.D. thesis of Jane Sillery, Oxford University, 1996.

7. *Foreign Relations of the United States 1961-1963*, Vol. XII, pp. 524 and 526: Schlesinger to Kennedy, 30 and 31 August, 1961, quoted in Sillery, loc. cit., pp. 84-85.

8. Public Record Office: PREM 11/3666 – Rusk to Home, 20 February 1962; Minute from Macmillan to Home initialled 'H.M. 21.2.62' and Home to Rusk, 26 February 1962, in S. R. Ashton and D. Killimgray (eds), *British Documents on the End of Empire*, Institute of Commonwealth Studies, London, pp. 486-7 and 494.

The Socialist History Society

The Socialist History Society was founded in 1992 and includes many leading Socialist and labour historians, both academic and amateur, in Britain and overseas. The SHS holds regular events, public meetings and one-off conferences, and contributes to current historical debates and controversies. The society produces a range of publications, including the journal *Socialist History.*

The SHS is the successor to the Communist Party History Group, established in 1946. The society is now independent of all political parties and groups. We are engaged in and seek to encourage historical studies from a Marxist and broadly-defined left perspective. We are concerned with every aspect of human history from early social formations to the present day and aim for a global reach.

We are particularly interested in the struggles of labour, women, progressive and peace movements throughout the world, as well as the movements and achievements of colonial peoples, black people, and other oppressed communities seeking justice, human dignity and liberation.

Each year we produce two issues of our journal *Socialist History,* one or two historical pamphlets in our *Occasional Papers* series, and members' newsletters. We hold a public lecture and debate in London five times per year. In addition, we organise occasional conferences, book-launch meetings, and joint events with other sympathetic groups.

Join the Socialist History Society!
Members receive all our serial publications for the year at no extra cost and regular mailings about our activities. Members can vote at our AGM and seek election to positions on the committee, and are encouraged to participate in other society activities.

Annual membership fees for 2012 (renewable every January):

Full UK	£25.00
Concessionary UK	£18.00
Europe full	£30.00
Europe concessionary	£24.00
Rest of world full	£35.00
Rest of world concessionary	£29.00

For details of institutional subscriptions, please e-mail the treasurer on francis@socialisthistorysociety.co.uk .

To join the society for 2012, please send your name and address plus a cheque/PO payable to **Socialist History Society** to: SHS, 50 Elmfield Road, Balham, London SW17 8AL. Subscriptions can also be paid online. Visit our websites on www.socialisthistorysociety.co.uk and www.socialist-history-journal.org.uk.

New from Bogle-L'Ouverture Press

Pulling the Punches - Defeating Domestic Violence

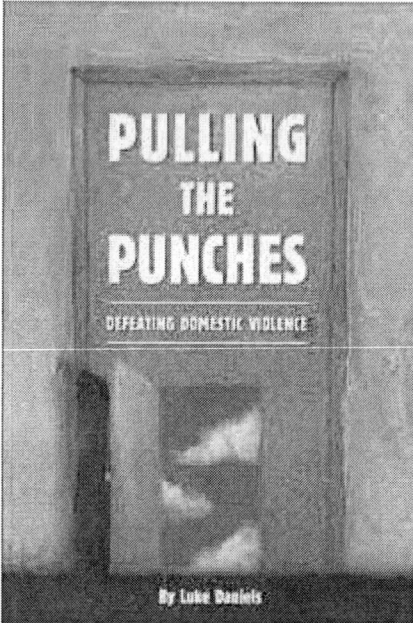

Pulling the Punches by Luke Daniels is the first book addressed to perpetrators of domestic violence who want to stop their violent behaviour. Survivors will also find much in it that will empower them and its helpful guidance will be invaluable to the family and loved ones of those with abusive partners.

In addition this book will be useful to educators, social workers, students, probation officers, nurses, doctors and counsellors. For everyone concerned with stopping the scourge of violence in all its manifestations and working for a better society, *Pulling the Punches* is a goldmine of information and encouragement.

Published by: Bogle-L'Ouverture Press, P.O. Box 2186, London W13 9ZQ

Copies can be purchased via the website: www.pullingthepunches.com for £12.95 including post and packaging for anywhere in the UK. Overseas copies cost £14.95 including postage and packing.